Let's Check Out the UK!

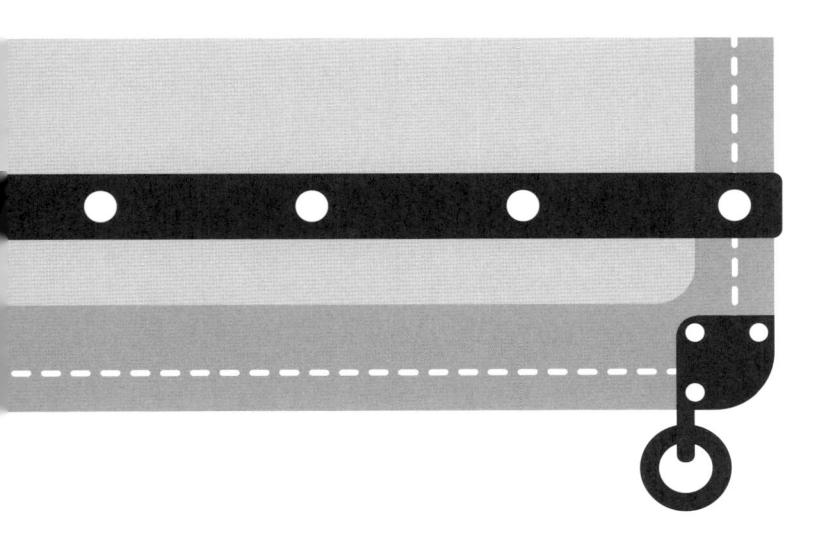

Paul Chris McVay
Nobumichi Kawada

KINSEIDO

Kinseido Publishing Co., Ltd.
3-21 Kanda Jimbo-cho, Chiyoda-ku,
Tokyo 101-0051, Japan

Copyright © 2015 by Paul Chris McVay
　　　　　　　　　Nobumichi Kawada

All rights reserved. No part of this publication may be reproduced, stored in a retrieval system, or transmitted, in any form or by any means, electronic, mechanical, photocopying, recording or otherwise, without the prior permission of the publisher.

First published 2015 by Kinseido Publishing Co., Ltd.

Design　　　　Nampoosha Co., Ltd.
Illustrations　Hayato Kamoshita

Photo credit
　Page 26　dpa/Jiji Press Photo
　Page 48　dpa/Jiji Press Photo
　Page 50　AFP/Jiji
　Page 62　dpa/Jiji Press Photo
　Page 70　AFP/Jiji

音声ファイル無料ダウンロード

https://www.kinsei-do.co.jp/download/4000

この教科書で DL 00 の表示がある箇所の音声は、上記URLまたはQRコードにて無料でダウンロードできます。自習用音声としてご活用ください。

▶ PCからのダウンロードをお勧めします。スマートフォンなどでダウンロードされる場合は、
　ダウンロード前に「解凍アプリ」をインストールしてください。
▶ URLは、検索ボックスではなくアドレスバー（URL表示欄）に入力してください。
▶ お使いのネットワーク環境によっては、ダウンロードできない場合があります。

◎ CD 00　左記の表示がある箇所の音声は、教室用CD（Class Audio CD）に収録されています。

Preface

Hi, Everyone!

My name's Chris McVay. I come from England, and it is my pleasure to serve as Takeshi's and, more importantly, YOUR guide on this short trip to the UK.

In this textbook, we want to give you a more unusual, 'behind-the-scenes', view of Britain, visiting different places and focusing on original themes.

The realistic dialogues, interesting readings and challenging exercises will help you improve your all-round English skills in a fun way.

So, are you ready for an exciting trip? Well, pack your bags and let's go and check out the UK!

Paul Chris McVay

はしがき

この教科書は、日本人大学生のタケシが、イギリス人のクリス先生と一緒に15日間のイギリス旅行に出る、という設定で作られています。

インターネットや雑誌、テレビなどを通してしかイギリスという国を知らない、という皆さんも多いと思います。実際に街を歩き、見て、聞き、イギリスの社会や美しい風景、歴史、そしてそこに暮らす人たちと出会うことができるこの旅に、タケシも期待でいっぱいのことでしょう。

タケシは、クリス先生との会話を楽しみながら、今までしたことのない経験や、たくさんの知識を得ていきます。皆さんも、２人と共にイギリス旅行をしているつもりになって、この国が持つさまざまな側面を見てみましょう。皆さんの知らないことがたくさんあるはずです。

クリス先生の視点で語られるリーディングも興味深く読めるでしょう。クリス先生はイギリス英語を話されるので、耳にするよい機会です。先生の真似をして実際に発音してみるのもよい勉強になります。また、大学生として必要な、語彙力や表現力を磨くための練習問題も用意されています。

さあ、クリス先生とタケシと一緒に、イギリス旅行に出かけましょう！

川田伸道

Let's Check Out the UK!

CONTENTS

General Information ……… 4
Map & Destinations ……… 5

Day 1   **I Can't Wait to Explore Britain!**
「イギリス」は英語で何て言う? ……… 8

Day 2   **How about Going to a Pub?**
パブカルチャーと飲酒問題 ……… 12

Day 3   **The Scenery Is Breathtaking, Isn't It?**
ナショナルトラストに守られる美しき湖水地方 ……… 16

Day 4   **What Do You Suggest We Do Today?**
雨の日には美術館へ ……… 20

Day 5   **This Is a Multi-Ethnic Country**
多民族社会イギリス ……… 24

Day 6   **What's It Like Being a Student in the UK?**
大学生でいるのも楽じゃない! ……… 30

Day 7   **Mmm... It Sounds Too Risky**
賭けてみる? ブックメーカーの行く末は ……… 34

Day 8   **You Should Try Fish and Chips!**
多彩で美味しい! イギリス料理 ……… 38

Day 9	**It's Fun Listening to Different Accents**
	8月のエディンバラ ································· 42

Day 10	**Do You Fancy Something Sweet?**
	そのチョコレート、原料はどこから？ ·············· 46

Day 11	**I Guess I Should Have a Black-Cab Experience**
	市内どこへも最短距離で！ロンドンタクシー ·········· 52

Day 12	**I'm Looking forward to Seeing Wales!**
	ウェールズ語とチャールズ皇太子 ················· 56

Day 13	**Don't You Know that UK Designs Are Popular?**
	カッコイイだけにあらず、ブリティッシュ・スタイル ······ 60

Day 14	**Would You Like to See a Play?**
	英語は詩人シェイクスピアに学べ ················· 64

Day 15	**That's the Great Thing about Travel!**
	変わりゆくイギリス王室 ························ 68

Names of People & Groups

- 28 ● 本書に登場する人名・団体名① (Day 3, 4 and 5)
- 50 ● 本書に登場する人名・団体名② (Day 8, 10 and 13)
- 72 ● 本書に登場する人名・団体名③ (Day 13, 14 and 15)

Let's Talk about the UK!

- 29 ● 英国コラム①
  3人のイギリス民間人が始めたナショナルトラスト運動
  自分好みの展示がきっと見つかる！ロンドンの美術館・博物館

- 51 ● 英国コラム②
  イギリスの大学での勉強やキャンパスライフ、日本との違い
  キャドバリーも取り組むフェアトレードって？

- 73 ● 英国コラム③
  ブラックキャブ、ダブルデッカーを乗りこなそう！
  プリンス・オブ・ウェールズって、結局どこの王子様？

General Information ｜イギリス一般情報｜

- ◆**国名**：グレートブリテン及び北アイルランド連合王国
  フレートブリテンにあたるイングランド、ウェールズ、スコットランドの3つと北アイルランドで構成されている。
- ◆**面積**：245,000km² (日本の約3分の2)
- ◆**人口**：推定6,370万人 (2012年調べ、日本の約半分)
  内訳は、イングランド5,300万人、ウェールズ310万人、スコットランド530万人、北アイルランド180万人。EU加盟国の中では、ドイツ、フランスに次いで3番目に人口が多い。
- ◆**首都**：ロンドン
- ◆**公用語**：英語 (ウェールズ語、スコットランド語、ゲール語)
- ◆**通貨**：スターリング・ポンド (£) と補助単位のペンス (p)

£1=100p=約172円 (2014年8月現在)。スコットランドや北アイルランド、マン島では独自の紙幣を発行している。価値はイングランドで発行されたものと同じで、イングランドでも使うことができる。

- ◆**政治体制**：立憲君主制、議院内閣制、EU (欧州連合) に加盟
  エリザベス女王はイギリスの元首。立憲君主制のもと、王室は政府に対して重要な儀式的・公的な役割を担っている。議会制民主主義をとっており、政府は国民によって5年ごとに選挙で選ばれ、閣僚と大臣の支持を受けて首相が政府を率いる。
- ◆**日本との時差**：マイナス9時間
  日本が午前7時の時、イギリスでは前日の午後10時である。サマータイム制度を採用しているためサマータイム期間中 (3月最終日曜日午前1時から10月最終日曜日午前1時まで) はマイナス8時間の時差になる。

ヒースロー空港からロンドン市内へ

　日本からの便はほぼすべてが、ロンドン西部にあるイギリス最大の空港、ロンドン・ヒースロー空港に降り立つ。国際線利用者数では世界一の空港。ロンドン市内へのアクセス方法は、列車、地下鉄、コーチバス、タクシーなどがある。

🚈 ヒースロー・エクスプレス [列車]
空港直結の駅からロンドン中心部に近いパディントン駅まで、約20分で結ぶ。15分間隔で早朝から深夜まで運行されている。料金はスタンダードクラスで片道大人20ポンド。

🚌 ナショナル・エクスプレス・コーチ [バス]
コーチと呼ばれるバスのサービスで、約40分でロンドン市内まで行ける。片道大人8ポンドで、空港から市内までのアクセス方法の中で一番安い。

4

Map & Destinations
地図

Scotland
- Inverness
- Aberdeen
- Fort William
- St. Andrews
- Glasgow
- Edinburgh

Northern Ireland
- Belfast

Ireland
- Dublin

England
- Newcastle-upon-Tyne
- Carlisle
- Lake District National Park
- Lancaster
- York
- Leeds
- Manchester
- Sheffield
- Liverpool
- Nottingham
- Norwich
- Birmingham
- Stratford-upon-Avon
- Cambridge
- Cotswolds
- Oxford
- Canterbury
- London
- Bristol
- Dover
- Portsmouth
- Brighton
- Isle of Wight
- St. Ives
- Plymouth

Wales
- Conwy
- Snowdonia National Park
- Swansea
- Cardiff
- Gower Peninsula
- Wye Valley

North Atlantic Ocean
North Sea
Irish Sea
Isle of Man

Map & Destinations

Day 3

Lake District National Park
〔湖水地方国立公園〕
イングランド北西部のカンブリア州に広がる2,292km²に及ぶイングランド最大の国立公園。16の湖や500以上の沼、国立自然保護区をかかえ、イギリスで最も人気の高い保養地となっている。

Lake Windermere 〔ウィンダミア湖〕
湖水地方の玄関口にあたるカンブリア州ウィンダミアにある湖。南北に細長い氷河湖でイングランド最大の面積をほこる。カヤック乗りやウィンドサーフィンなどが楽しめる。

Scafell Pike 〔スコーフェル山〕
湖水地方にある標高978mの山で、イングランド最高峰。

Lake Windermere, Cumbria

Day 9

Edinburgh
〔エディンバラ、スコットランドの首都〕
東のフォース湾に面し、グラスゴーにつぐスコットランド第2の都市で、政治の中心。旧市街と新市街の美しい町並みが世界遺産に登録されている。8月に開催される芸術的な祭典が有名。

Loch Lomond 〔ローモンド湖〕
グラスゴーの北に位置する、表面積ではスコットランド最大の淡水湖。周囲は国立公園になっている。

Loch Ness 〔ネス湖〕
スコットランド北西部にある細長い淡水湖。怪獣ネッシーがすむという言い伝えがあることで知られる。

Edinburgh Castle at nightfall

Day 12

Cardiff 〔カーディフ、ウェールズの首都〕
ヨーロッパで一番新しい首都ではあるが、古城がたくさん残っており、歴史を感じさせてくれる街でもある。中心部にはカーディフ城があり、コッホ城、トゥムパス城などの見学ができる。

Snowdonia National Park
〔スノードニア国立公園〕
ウェールズ北西部のにある、ウェールズで最も高い1,085mのスノードン山を中心とした山岳地帯一体に広がる国立公園。荘厳な中世の古城と豊かな自然の調和がとれた美しいエリア。

the Gower Peninsula 〔ガウアー半島〕
ウェールズ南部に位置する、特別自然美観地域。石灰岩の崖や手つかずの美しい海岸が人気。

Entrance to the old town in Cardiff

Wye Valley 〔ワイ渓谷〕
イングランドとウェールズの国境に位置する風光明媚な地域で、大部分は特別自然美観地域に指定されている。イギリスの観光業発祥の地とも言われ、ワーズワースなどの文人や画家たちも訪れている。

Castles of Beaumaris, Harlech, Caenarfon, and Conwy
〔ボーマリス城、ハーレフ城、カーナヴォン城、コンウィ城〕
エドワード１世がウェールズのイングランド化対策のために建てた城。1986年に世界遺産に登録。

Llanfairpwllgwyngyllgogerychwyrndrobwllllantysiliogogogoch
〔ランヴァイル・プルグウィンギル・ゴゲリフウィルンドロブル・ランティシリオゴゴゴホ〕
ウェールズ北部のアングルシー島にある村の名前。ウェールズ語で「赤い洞窟の聖ティシリオ教会のそばの激しい渦巻きの近くの白いハシバミの森の泉のほとりにある聖マリア教会」という意味になる。

Day 14

Stratford-upon-Avon
〔ストラトフォード・アポン・エイヴォン〕
シェイクスピアの故郷として有名で、劇場や生家のあった場所など、シェイクスピアに関連する施設や美しい田園風景を楽しむことができる。

Cotswolds 〔コッツウォルズ〕
標高300mに位置する、「羊の丘」という意味の古い歴史のある丘陵地帯。蜂蜜色の石を積み上げた特徴的な建物で知られる。

Quaint town in the Cotswolds

LONDON ロンドンの風景

（左上）
The River Thames and the Houses of Parliament
（右上）
Underground station entrance
（左下）
Camden Market
（右下）
Double decker and black cab

Map & Destinations 7

Day 1

I Can't Wait to Explore Britain!
「イギリス」は英語で何て言う？

日本人大学生のタケシが、大学のクリス先生と一緒に
イギリスはロンドンのヒースロー空港に到着しました。
タケシがずっと楽しみにしていた15日間のイギリス旅行の始まりです！
イギリスの国名は、日本語では正式には
「グレートブリテン及び北アイルランド連合王国」です。
さて、英語では何と呼ぶか、知っていますか。

Listen to the Dialogue

DL 02　CD 02

会話文の音声を聞いて、空所に適切な語を書き入れましょう。
完成したら、ペアになって会話の練習をしてみましょう。

Chris: Welcome to the UK, Takeshi!
Takeshi: Thanks, Chris. It's great to be here at last.
Chris: I know you've been [1.]_____ _____ visit Britain for such a long time, right?
Takeshi: Yes, it's been my dream since secondary school.
Chris: So how do you feel?
Takeshi: A bit nervous, but very [2.]_____!
Chris: OK, let's get our bags.
Takeshi: Wow, Heathrow Airport is [3.]_____ _____.
Chris: It's actually the third busiest airport in the world. It has 5 terminals.
Takeshi: Mmm, that's interesting. How do we [4.]_____ _____ central London?
Chris: I suggest catching the Heathrow Express. It's the fastest way. [5.]_____ _____ only 15 minutes.
Takeshi: Fine. I can't wait to explore Britain and learn more about the British way of life [6.]_____ _____.
Chris: That's what we've come for, so let's start!

Notes be dying to ...「〜したくて仕方がない」　secondary school「中等学校」　explore「〜を探検する・見て回る」　nervous「気持ちが高ぶる、緊張する」　way of life「生活様式」　That's what we've come for「そのために私たちはやって来た」

▶▶▶ 4ページの『一般情報』も参照

Expressions for Everyday English

Let's ＋動詞の原形「～しましょう」「さあ～しよう」

何かをしようと誘ったり、提案する際に用いる表現で、主語が省略されています。let's は、let us の短縮形で、動詞の原形を伴い「私たちに～させてくれ」という意味になります。そこから「～しよう」という意味で使われます。

🎧 DL 03　💿 CD 03

Let's play tennis.　テニスをしましょう。
Let's go to the zoo.　動物園に行こうよ。
Let's eat out tonight.　今夜は外食にしよう。
Let's look at some examples.　例をいくつか見てみましょう。

Let's Try!

学習した表現を使って自由に英文を作り、ペアになって会話をしてみましょう。
A: The weather is really nice today.　今日は本当に天気が良いなあ。
B: Let's _____.　_____ しようよ。

Useful Vocabulary

🎧 DL 04　💿 CD 04

以下は、次ページで学習するトピックに関する重要語句です。
それぞれの語句の意味に当てはまる日本語を、選択肢から選びましょう。

1. confusing　　　[　　]
2. clear up　　　[　　]
3. refer to　　　[　　]
4. be made up of　[　　]
5. along with　　[　　]
6. even though　　[　　]
7. accurate　　　[　　]
8. upset　　　　[　　]
9. identity　　　[　　]
10. be proud of　　[　　]

> **a.** ～のことを言う・呼ぶ　**b.** ～と一緒に、～に加えて
> **c.** ～で構成された　**d.** 混乱させる　**e.** ～を誇りに思う　**f.** 正確な
> **g.** ～をはっきりさせる　**h.** 憤慨して　**i.** 主体性　**j.** ～だけれども

Day 1　I Can't Wait to Explore Britain!

Reading: Chris's Insight

Welcome to the UK... Great Britain... the British Isles... Huh?

The UK, Great Britain, Britain, the British Isles... It's all so **confusing**, even for some Brits! Let's try to **clear** things **up** a little bit.
5 The United Kingdom **refers to** the union of England, Scotland, Wales and Northern Ireland. In fact, the UK's official name is the 'United Kingdom of Great Britain and
10 Northern Ireland'. Great Britain, or simply Britain, **is made up of** England, Scotland and Wales. The British Isles is a geographical term for the two large islands of Great Britain and Ireland **along with** 5,000 smaller islands. Now do you understand? Good. But the British Olympic Association calls its team 'Team GB' **even though** it
15 includes athletes from Northern Ireland. How strange! Many people think it would be more **accurate** to call it 'Team UK'.

A man with 'Team GB' logo on his back

But no matter how confused you may be, one very important point to remember is never to call people from Scotland, Wales, or Northern Ireland 'English'! They may get **upset**, as they have separate **identities** and **are** very **proud**
20 **of** their own history and cultural traditions, and even their own languages! However, it is safe to call them 'British', since all countries are united under the same flag, the Union Jack.

Notes Brits「イギリス人」 the 'United Kingdom of Great Britain and Northern Ireland'「グレートブリテン及び北部アイルランド連合王国」 geographical「地理学的な」 the British Olympic Association「イギリスオリンピック委員会」 'Team GB'「イギリス代表チーム」 no matter how ... = however...「どんなに〜でも」(*No matter how* hard I try, I can't figure out computers.「どんなに頑張ってやってみても、コンピューターがわからない」) the Union Jack イギリスの国旗。Union Flagともいう。

Reading Comprehension

本文の内容に合わせて、質問の答えとして正しいものを選択肢から選びましょう。

1. What is the difference between the UK and Great Britain?
   a. There is no difference
   b. The UK includes Northern Ireland
   c. The UK is the official name

2. What is strange about the name 'Team GB'?
   a. It doesn't recognise athletes from Northern Ireland
   b. It is not supported by the British Olympic Association
   c. It is more accurate than 'Team UK'

3. Why is it not good to call all British people 'English'?
   a. Because it is confusing
   b. Because many people may get upset
   c. Because they have the same Union Jack flag

Writing Exercises

本章中で使われている表現を参考にして、以下の英文を完成させましょう。

1. 娘は長くてきれいな髪の毛が自慢です。
   My daughter _____ _____ of her beautiful long hair.

2. 外国語をマスターするには長い時間がかかります。
   It _____ a long _____ to master a foreign language.

3. 父は風邪をひいているのに、仕事に行きました。
   My father went to work _____ _____ he had a cold.

4. 弟はクラスで2番目に背が低いです。
   My little brother is _____ _____ shortest in his class.

Day 2: How about Going to a Pub?

パブカルチャーと飲酒問題

朝からロンドンの街を歩き回った様子のクリス先生とタケシ。
そろそろお昼の時間のようです。
イギリスのパブは、ランチタイムも営業していて、ソフトドリンクはもちろん、
名物のフィッシュ＆チップスなど、美味しい料理を楽しむこともできます。
パブは、イギリス文化のひとつとも言えます。
イギリスが抱える飲酒問題についても学んでみましょう。

Listen to the Dialogue

DL 07　CD 07

会話文の音声を聞いて、空所に適切な語を書き入れましょう。
完成したら、ペアになって会話の練習をしてみましょう。

Chris: We've seen so many amazing 1._____ this morning.

Takeshi: Yeah, but now I need a break. My feet are 2._____ _____, and I'm soooo thirsty.

Chris: Me too. Look, there's a pub just across the street. How about going there?

Takeshi: Will it be open 3._____ _____ _____ of the day?

Chris: Of course. Pubs have been allowed to stay open all day for quite a 4._____ _____ now.

Takeshi: Oh, I didn't know that. Anyway, it's too early to drink alcohol, and I want to eat something. I'm starving!

Chris: Don't worry. Most pubs 5._____ soft drinks and, nowadays, even tea and coffee. They also have very tasty food 6._____ _____ 'pub grub'.

Takeshi: In that case, it sounds perfect! Let's go!

Notes a break「休憩」　pub = public house「パブ・酒場」　have been allowed to...「〜することが許可された」　all day「一日中」　starving「腹ぺこで」　in that case「もしそうなら」

Expressions for Everyday English

How about (-ing)?「(〜するの) はいかがですか」

話者（尋ねている人）が相手に何かを提案したり、勧めたりする際に使う表現です。前置詞の about の後は名詞、または動名詞（-ing）が入ります。

DL 08　CD 08

How about having lunch at a pub?　パブでランチをとるのはどうですか。

How about going for a walk?　散歩に行ってはいかがですか。

How about some wine with your meal?　お食事と一緒にワインはいかがですか。

How about taking a taxi instead?
　　　　　　　　　（車や電車などの）代わりにタクシーに乗るのはいかがですか。

Let's Try!

学習した表現を使って自由に英文を作り、ペアになって会話をしてみましょう。

A: What do you want to eat for dinner today?　今夜は夕食に何を食べたいですか。

B: How about _____？ _____はどうですか。

Useful Vocabulary

DL 09　CD 09

以下は、次ページで学習するトピックに関する重要語句です。
それぞれの語句の意味に当てはまる日本語を、選択肢から選びましょう。

1. surprising　　[　]　　6. unfortunately　[　]
2. excellent　　 [　]　　7. huge amount　　[　]
3. value　　　　[　]　　8. pass　　　　　　[　]
4. comment　　 [　]　　9. prevent　　　　[　]
5. cosy　　　　 [　]　　10. work　　　　　[　]

> **a.** 非常に多くの量　**b.** 驚くべき、意外な　**c.** すばらしい
> **d.** 〜を防ぐ　**e.** 価値　**f.** 機能する　**g.** 〜と評する
> **h.** （議案などが）通過する　**i.** くつろげる　**j.** 不幸にも

Day 2　How about Going to a Pub?

Reading: Chris's Insight

Britain's Pubs Welcome You

One of the first things a visitor to Britain notices is that there is a pub on almost every street corner. This is not ***surprising*** as there are over 50,000 of them in the UK! The British pub dates back to Roman times and is still a central part of British life and culture. Many people say that if you haven't been to a pub, you haven't really experienced Britain. Tourists from all over the world not only enjoy the ***excellent*** beer and good ***value*** food, but also ***comment*** on the ***cosy***, welcoming atmosphere of pubs. Total strangers will often begin a conversation with you while you are waiting to order at the bar.

Crown & Anchor, English pub in London.

This all sounds fun, but ***unfortunately*** there is a negative side to the picture: Britain is known as the binge-drinking capital of Europe[*]. This means that although Brits do not generally drink as much as other Europeans, some tend to drink a ***huge amount*** in a short time. A new law was ***passed*** in 2005 allowing pubs to stay open longer in order to ***prevent*** binge-drinking, but it has not ***worked***. So, enjoy the British pub scene but be careful of drunks, especially at the weekend!

＊2010年欧州委員会の調査より

Notes on almost every street corner「街中いたるところに」 dates back to「〜にさかのぼる」 total strangers「まったく知らない人たち」 picture「状況」 binge-drinking「酒浸りの、度が過ぎる飲酒の」 capital「中心地」 drunks「泥酔した人たち」

Reading Comprehension

本文の内容に合わせて、質問の答えとして正しいものを選択肢から選びましょう。

1. What do visitors quickly notice about Britain?
   a. There are many Roman ruins
   b. There are tourists from around the world
   c. There are lots of pubs

2. How much alcohol do some Brits drink?
   a. A very large quantity at one time
   b. More than other Europeans
   c. Not much at weekends

3. Why was a new law passed in 2005?
   a. To stop binge drinking
   b. To allow people to drink more
   c. To take care of drunks

Writing Exercises

本章中で使われている表現を参考にして、以下の英文を完成させましょう。

1. 日本人は塩分を摂り過ぎる傾向にあります。
   Japanese _____ _____ consume too much salt.

2. 彼の家は、居心地がいいだけでなく、温かな雰囲気があります。
   His house is not _____ cosy, but also has a warm _____.

3. ステラはあまりにも内気で、男性に話しかけることができません。
   Stella is _____ shy _____ speak to men.

4. このテストでは、辞書の使用が認められています。
   You are _____ _____ use a dictionary for this test.

Day 2　How about Going to a Pub?　15

Day 3

The Scenery Is Breathtaking, Isn't It?

ナショナルトラストに守られる美しき湖水地方

イングランド北西部に位置する湖水地方。
その優美な地形で知られる美しい景観は、風情のある街並みと共に
多くの人々を魅了してきました。
ここは『ピーター・ラビットのおはなし』の舞台としてよく知られていますが、
歴史的建築物や自然景勝地の保護を目的とした
「ナショナルトラスト」の象徴的な地域でもあります。

Listen to the Dialogue

DL 12　CD 12

会話文の音声を聞いて、空所に適切な語を書き入れましょう。
完成したら、ペアになって会話の練習をしてみましょう。

Chris: Here we are – the famous Lake District National Park. It's ¹._____ _____ national park in Britain.

Takeshi: Wow! The scenery is breathtaking, isn't it?

Chris: Absolutely!

Takeshi: I can see lots of people windsurfing on the lake. I fancy ²._____ that.

Chris: That's Lake Windermere, the biggest of the 16 lakes in the park. You can ³._____ _____ _____ at windsurfing tomorrow, but today, we're ⁴._____ _____ climb England's highest mountain – Scafell Pike. It's 978 metres high.

Takeshi: Ha! Do you call that a mountain? Mt Fuji is 3,776 metres high.

Chris: Wait until you try climbing it – you'll see! Oh, I recommend ⁵._____ this umbrella.

Takeshi: But it's sunny.

Chris: In Britain, we can have ⁶._____ _____ in one day! And the Lake District is the wettest area in the country.

Notes Lake District「湖水地方」イングランド北西部に位置する保養地。　Lake Windermere「ウィンダミア湖」　Scafell Pike「スコーフェル山」

▶▶▶ 5、6ページも参照

Expressions for Everyday English

be going to ＋動詞の原形「～する予定です」「～するつもりです」

「(前から計画していたこと、決まっていたことを) するでしょう、する予定です」という場合に用います。未来のことを述べる際に用いる助動詞 will は、あらかじめ決まっている予定ではなく、単に予測する場合に用います。

DL 13　CD 13

I'm going to need your help.　これからあなたの力が必要となります。
We're going to be in town until Friday.　私たちは金曜まで町に滞在する予定です。
I'm going to leave at eight.　8時に出発します。
It will rain tomorrow.　明日雨が降るでしょう。[単に未来のことを言っている]

Let's Try!

学習した表現を使って自由に英文を作り、ペアになって会話をしてみましょう。

A: What are you going to do today?　今日は何をする？
B: I'm going to _____ . _____ するつもりだよ。

Useful Vocabulary

DL 14　CD 14

以下は、次ページで学習するトピックに関する重要語句です。
それぞれの語句の意味に当てはまる日本語を、選択肢から選びましょう。

1. scenic　　　　　　[　]
2. organisation　　　[　]
3. preserve　　　　　[　]
4. charge　　　　　　[　]
5. renowned　　　　 [　]
6. destination　　　　[　]
7. learn by heart　　　[　]
8. illustrate　　　　　[　]
9. throughout　　　　[　]
10. guaranteed　　　　[　]

　　a. ～を暗記する　　b. 料金　　c. ～のあらゆる場所で　　d. 組織
　　e. 有名な　　f. 眺めの美しい　　g. ～に挿絵を入れる　　h. 目的地
　　i. 保証されて　　j. ～を保護する

Day 3　The Scenery Is Breathtaking, Isn't It?

Reading: Chris's Insight

The Lake District and the National Trust

The Lake District ranks highly among the many beautiful spots to visit in Britain. It is recognised worldwide for its natural beauty, with magnificent lakes, rocky mountains, and **scenic** valleys. Many areas of Britain, like the Lake District, are protected by the National Trust, a non-profit conservation **organisation**. The National Trust also **preserves** historic houses and gardens. Many can be visited free of **charge** and are extremely well supported by the British public.

The Lake District is equally **renowned** for its writers. The 19th-century poet William Wordsworth spent most of his life in the Lake District and his three homes are now popular tourist **destinations**. English schoolchildren used to **learn by heart** his most famous poem, 'I Wandered Lonely as a Cloud'. I can still remember it today! Beatrix Potter wrote and **illustrated** many of her children's stories in her Lake District home, Hill Top, which is protected by the National Trust. Her best-known book, 'The Tale of Peter Rabbit', is loved **throughout** the world, including Japan.

Whether you're active and are into hiking and watersports or you like literature and history, you are **guaranteed** a wonderful time in the Lake District — but don't forget to take an umbrella!

Dove Cottage, a house in the Lake District where Wordsworth wrote much of his poetry, including 'I Wandered Lonely as a Cloud'

Notes the National Trust「ナショナルトラスト」非営利の自然保護・歴史的建造物維持を目的とした団体。　conservation「保護」　William Wordsworth　ウィリアム・ワーズワース (1770-1850)。詩人。　'I Wandered Lonely as a Cloud'　ワーズワース作の『水仙』(1804)。　Beatrix Potter　ビアトリクス・ポター (1886-1943)。絵本作家。　Hill Top「ヒル・トップ」ポターが晩年住んだ家。　'The Tale of Peter Rabbit'『ピーター・ラビットのおはなし』(1902)。ポター作の児童書。　are into...「〜に関心を持って・夢中で」

▶▶ 28ページの『本書に登場する人名・団体名』、および29ページのコラムも参照

Reading Comprehension

本文の内容に合わせて、質問の答えとして正しいものを選択肢から選びましょう。

1. What is the Lake District well known for all over the world?
   a. For its high mountains
   b. For the National Trust
   c. For its natural beauty and its famous writers

2. What connection do Wordsworth and Beatrix Potter have with the Lake District?
   a. They taught schoolchildren there
   b. They both had homes there
   c. They made it popular in Japan

3. What should you always take when you visit the Lake District?
   a. An umbrella
   b. Hiking boots
   c. A swimming costume

Writing Exercises

本章中で使われている表現を参考にして、以下の英文を完成させましょう。

1. 京都には見るべき所がたくさんあります。
   There are many _____ _____ see in Kyoto.

2. 今週末、映画に行きたいですか。
   Do you _____ _____ to the cinema this weekend?

3. 昔は、よくテニスをしたものですが、今はあまりしていません。
   I _____ _____ play tennis a lot, but I don't play much now.

4. あなたは単語や句をたくさん暗記しなければなりません。
   You have to _____ many words and phrases _____ _____ .

Day 4

What Do You Suggest We Do Today?

雨の日には美術館へ

ロンドンと言えば雨。
今日も朝から天気が悪く、ガッカリした様子のタケシに、
クリス先生がミュージアム訪問を提案しました。
世界的に有名な大英博物館から、住宅街にある小さなものまで、
ロンドンにあるミュージアムの種類は豊富。
美術館めぐりは、旅先での優雅な時間の使い方です。

Listen to the Dialogue

DL 18　CD 18

会話文の音声を聞いて、空所に適切な語を書き入れましょう。
完成したら、ペアになって会話の練習をしてみましょう。

Takeshi: Oh, no! It's raining cats and dogs.
Chris: Don't worry, Takeshi. There's lots to do in London on 1._____ _____.
Takeshi: So, what do you suggest we do today?
Chris: Well, we haven't been to 2._____ _____ London's famous museums yet.
Takeshi: That's true. But today is Sunday. They'll be closed, won't they?
Chris: No. The good news is that 3._____ _____ museums are open seven days a week.
Takeshi: That's wonderful.
Chris: And the 4._____ _____ news is that most of them are free.
Takeshi: You're kidding, aren't you?
Chris: Absolutely not.
Takeshi: Unbelievable! Londoners are 5._____ _____.
Chris: I agree. Now, I think we should go to the British Museum first, and then to the Tate Modern if we have 6._____ _____ left.
Takeshi: Sounds good. Let's go!

Notes　It's raining cats and dogs.「雨が激しく降っている」　Absolutely not.「とんでもない」　Londoners「ロンドン市民、ロンドン子」　the British Museum「大英博物館」世界最大の博物館のひとつ。ロゼッタストーンなど世界各国の貴重な発掘物や美術工芸品の展示で知られる。　the Tate Modern「テイト・モダン」テムズ川沿いに位置するサウス・バンク地区にある国立の近現代美術館。

Expressions for Everyday English

~, don't you? / ~, aren't you?「～ですよね」「～ですか」（付加疑問）

文末に疑問文を付けて、同意を求める、または確認や質問をする表現です。肯定文には否定の、否定文には肯定の疑問文をつけ、命令文には ~, will you?、Let's で始まる文には ~, shall we? をつけます。語尾を下げる〈↘〉と同意を求めた文に、上げる〈↗〉と確認や質問の意味を含めた文になります。

🎧 DL 19　💿 CD 19

He is good at Spanish, isn't he?　彼はスペイン語が上手ですよね？〈↘〉

You didn't take a picture of them, did you?　彼らの写真を撮ってないよね？〈↘〉

Let's watch TV, shall we?　テレビを見ませんか？〈↗〉[Let's~]

Come for me at eight o'clock, will you?　8時に迎えに来てくれる？〈↗〉[命令文]

Let's Try!

学習した表現を使って自由に英文を作り、ペアになって会話をしてみましょう。

A: ＿＿＿＿＿＿＿＿＿, ＿＿＿＿＿＿＿＿＿? ＿＿＿＿＿＿＿＿＿?

B: Well, I don't know. さあ、分かりません。　Yes, I think so. ええ、そう思います。

Useful Vocabulary

🎧 DL 20　💿 CD 20

以下は、次ページで学習するトピックに関する重要語句です。
それぞれの語句の意味に当てはまる日本語を、選択肢から選びましょう。

1. interest　　　[　　]
2. cater to　　　[　　]
3. taste　　　　[　　]
4. attract　　　[　　]
5. fund　　　　[　　]
6. further　　　[　　]
7. exciting　　　[　　]
8. steadily　　　[　　]
9. be tired of　　[　　]
10. statement　　[　　]

a. もっと遠く　**b.** ～に資金を出す　**c.** ～に飽きる　**d.** 好み、し好
e. 意見、言葉　**f.** ～を満足させる　**g.** ワクワクするような
h. （興味など）を引きつける　**i.** 興味、関心　**j.** 着実に

Day 4　What Do You Suggest We Do Today?

Reading: Chris's Insight

DL 21, 22　CD 21　CD 22

UK Museums Will Never Bore You

Everyone knows it rains a lot in London, so it's only natural that there should be lots of things to do even on wet days. One of the
5　best activities is to visit a museum. There are over 240 museums in London, so, whatever your *interest* may be, you will surely be able to find a few that *cater*
10　*to* your *taste*. There are many small museums like the Sherlock Holmes Museum, the Cartoon Museum, and even the Chocolate Museum. Naturally, however, most visitors are *attracted* to the world-famous museums such as the British Museum, the Victoria and Albert Museum, and the
15　National Gallery. Luckily, these are among the many museums throughout Britain that are *funded* by the government, so they are free.

The entrance of the British Museum in London

Museums used to have an old, dusty, boring image. But nowadays, nothing could be *further* from the truth. They offer many *exciting* hands-on experiences for people of all ages. The British Museum attracts around 500,000
20　visitors a month, and all museums have grown *steadily* in popularity in recent years. Samuel Johnson once said: 'When a man *is tired of* London, he is tired of life'. London's many museums play a big role in keeping this *statement* true.

Notes　whatever... = no matter what...「〜は何でも、〜は皆」　surely「きっと、疑いなく」　nothing could be further from the truth「それ以上に真実から遠いものは何もない＝それはまるで見当違いである」　hands-on experience「実地体験」　around 500,000 visitors a month「1ヶ月につき約50万人の見学者」aは「〜につき、〜ごとに」の意味になる。　Samuel Johnson サミュエル・ジョンソン (1709-1784)。イギリスの文学者、詩人、評論家。

▶▶ 28ページの『本書に登場する人名・団体名』、および29ページのコラムも参照

22

Reading Comprehension

本文の内容に合わせて、質問の答えとして正しいものを選択肢から選びましょう。

1. Who do London's museums appeal to?
   a. People who don't like the rain
   b. All kinds of people
   c. Just a few people of good taste

2. Why are many museums free?
   a. Because there are so many of them
   b. Because they are world-famous
   c. Because they receive money from the government

3. How have museums changed their boring image?
   a. They have become more interactive
   b. They have grown in popularity
   c. They have supported what Samuel Johnson said

Writing Exercises

本章中で使われている表現を参考にして、以下の英文を完成させましょう。

1. いつかこの本を読みたいです。
   I want _____ _____ this book someday.

2. 教育は、社会で重要な役割を果たしています。
   Education _____ an important _____ in society.

3. キャシーがまだ到着していないとは変ですね。
   _____ is strange _____ Kathy hasn't arrived yet.

4. 学食で食べるのには飽きました。
   I am _____ _____ _____ at the school cafeteria.

Day 4　What Do You Suggest We Do Today?

Day 5: This Is a Multi-Ethnic Country

多民族社会イギリス

街歩きの途中で休憩中のクリス先生とタケシ。
通りを行き交う人たちの人種は、実にさまざまで
イギリスが多民族国家であることを実感させられます。
ロンドンなどの都市部の多民族化は、いまやアメリカ以上とも言われ、
有名人も含め、多種多様な民族的背景を持った人たちが暮らしています。
しかしそこには、いくつかの異なった価値観も存在するようです。

Listen to the Dialogue

DL 23　CD 23

会話文の音声を聞いて、空所に適切な語を書き入れましょう。
完成したら、ペアになって会話の練習をしてみましょう。

Chris: It's 1._____ _____ to sit down after all that walking.

Takeshi: Absolutely. You know, I love people-watching, and one thing that fascinates me 2._____ _____ is the variety of people you see.

Chris: Well, this is a multi-ethnic country, so there are people from practically 3._____ _____ in the world here.

Takeshi: I love that about Britain. It's so colourful and exciting.

Chris: Yes, Team GB at the London Olympics included Brits from many 4._____ backgrounds.

Takeshi: I guess it shows that immigration has been positive for Britain.

Chris: That's right. Now, 5._____ _____ a minute. I need to go to the loo.

Takeshi: The loo?

Chris: That's British English for the restroom.

Takeshi: Oh, I see.

Chris: Would you mind 6._____ my bag until I get back?

Takeshi: No problem.

Notes fascinates「〜の心を捉える、〜を魅了する」　multi-ethnic「多民族の」　backgrounds「(民族的)背景」　immigration「移住、移民」

Expressions for Everyday English

Would you mind -ing?「～していただけますか」(依頼)、「～してもよいでしょうか」(許可)

英語に敬語はありませんが、wouldを使うことで丁寧な表現になります。「～を気にする」という意味のmindの後は動名詞（-ing）を続け、答えがYesの場合は「気にします」、Noは「気にしません」という意味を表します。日本語の「はい／いいえ」の意味に影響されないようにしましょう。

🎧 DL 24　💿 CD 24

Would you mind telling me your name?　お名前を教えていただけますか。
Would you mind showing me the way?　道をお教え願えませんか。
Would you mind calling again later?　あとでまた電話してくれませんか。
Would you mind taking our photo?　写真を撮っていただけますか。
　Yes, I would.　いえ、できません。　No, I wouldn't.　ええ、構いませんよ。

Let's Try!
学習した表現を使って自由に英文を作り、ペアになって会話をしてみましょう。
A: Would you mind _____ ? _____ してくれますか。
B: Yes, _____ . いいえ、_____ 。　No, _____ . はい、_____ 。

Useful Vocabulary

🎧 DL 25　💿 CD 25

以下は、次ページで学習するトピックに関する重要語句です。
それぞれの語句の意味に当てはまる日本語を、選択肢から選びましょう。

1. ethnic group　　[　　]　　6. racial　　　　　[　　]
2. quite　　　　　[　　]　　7. tension　　　　[　　]
3. flow　　　　　[　　]　　8. discrimination　[　　]
4. lead to　　　　[　　]　　9. threat　　　　　[　　]
5. prejudice　　　[　　]　　10. thankfully　　　[　　]

---

a. かなり、なかなかの　**b.** 偏見　**c.** 脅威、危険なもの　**d.** 民族（民族集団）
e. 人種間の　**f.** （人やものの）流入、流れ　**g.** 緊張
h. ありがたいことに　**i.** 差別　**j.** ～を引き起こす、～につながる

Day 5　This Is a Multi-Ethnic Country

Reading: Chris's Insight

Britain - a Multi-Ethnic Society

One thing that stands out in Britain, especially in London, is the wide variety of **ethnic groups**. It is like a melting pot of the world. This is **quite** a change from the late 1940s when almost everyone you saw on the streets was white. Since that time, there has been a constant **flow** of immigrants into Britain from all corners of the world. At first, this **led to** a great deal of **prejudice** and violence, but gradually people came to see the advantages of immigration.

Now, the modern generation of Brits thinks less of race than their parents or grandparents. They went to school with kids of different races, so most have a mixed group of friends, and there are many mixed marriages nowadays. Also, many of their sporting or music 'heroes' come from different ethnic backgrounds: Lewis Hamilton, Danny Welbeck, Leona Lewis, Zayn Malik, and so many others. However, this does not mean that **racial tensions** and **discrimination** have completely disappeared from British society today. Sadly, some people still view immigrants as a **threat** to the British way of life. **Thankfully**, though, more people see them as an essential element of Britain's identity.

Zayn Malik (right) and Louis Tomlinson of One Direction

Notes stands out「際立つ、目につく」 melting pot「(人種・文化などの)るつぼ」種々のものや人が混じり合っている状態や場所のこと。 mixed marriages「異民族(異人種)間の結婚」 Lewis Hamilton ルイス・ハミルトン (1985-)。F1ドライバー。 Danny Welbeck ダニー・ウェルベック (1990-)。サッカー選手。 Leona Lewis レオナ・ルイス (1985-)。歌手。 Zayn Malik ゼイン・マリク (1993-)。歌手。
▶▶ 28ページの『本書に登場する人名・団体名』も参照

Reading Comprehension

本文の内容に合わせて、質問の答えとして正しいものを選択肢から選びましょう。

1. Why can Britain be considered a melting pot of the world?
   a. Because many people visit Britain
   b. Because people of many races live there
   c. Because many people have changed since the 1940s

2. What has happened in Britain since the 50s?
   a. Many immigrants have entered the UK
   b. There has been lots of violence
   c. More white people have appeared on the streets

3. What is the attitude of the majority of Brits towards immigrants today?
   a. They think immigrants are heroes
   b. They think immigrants cause racial tension
   c. They think immigrants are an important part of the British identity

Writing Exercises

本章中で使われている表現を参考にして、以下の英文を完成させましょう。

1. 喫煙は多くの健康上の問題を引き起こします。
   Smoking _____ _____ lots of health problems.

2. 今朝、オードリーから来た手紙はどこにある？
   _____ is the letter that _____ from Audrey this morning?

3. 多くの市民が彼を英雄視しています。
   Many citizens _____ him _____ a hero.

4. エマが仕事に費やす時間は、遊びの時間よりも短いです。
   Emma spends _____ time at work _____ on going out.

Day 5 This Is a Multi-Ethnic Country

Names of People & Groups

本書に登場する人名・団体名①

Day 3

William Wordsworth
ウィリアム・ワーズワース（1770-1850）

イギリスの代表的なロマン派詩人。故郷である湖水地方の美しい自然をこよなく愛し、自然讃美の詩を多数発表した。ヨーロッパ各地を点々とした後は生涯を湖水地方に暮らし、自然とともに生きた。『水仙』The Daffodilsは、湖水地方のアルスウォーター（Ullswater）湖のほとりを歩いていた際に見た、湖畔に沿って一面に咲く水仙の美しさに心を打たれて書いた詩と言われる。

Beatrix Potter
ビアトリクス・ポター（1886-1943）

『ピーターラビットのおはなし』シリーズで知られる、ロンドン出身の絵本作家。湖水地方の自然に魅了されたうちの一人で、美しい風景を守るために印税や遺産などの私財を投じ、ナショナルトラストの活動に大きく影響を与えた。

Day 4

Samuel Johnson
サミュエル・ジョンソン（1709-1784）

イギリスの文学者、詩人、評論家。1755年に、一人で編纂した『英語辞典』A Dictionary of the English Languageを刊行する。単語の意味を説明するために著名な作品の文章を引用した手法は、後続の辞典編纂に大きな影響を与えた。「ロンドンに飽きた者は人生に飽きた者だ。ロンドンには人生が与え得るものすべてがあるから」などの有名な警句から「典型的なイギリス人」と呼ばれる。

Day 5

Lewis Hamilton
ルイス・ハミルトン（1985- ）

F1ドライバー。アフリカ系イギリス人の父親とイングランド人の母親を持つ。2007年のデビュー戦では「F1史上初の黒人ドライバー」として注目を浴びた。

Danny Welbeck
ダニー・ウェルベック（1990- ）

両親をガーナ人に持つ、イングランド生まれのサッカー選手。地元のマンチェスター・ユナイテッドFCのアカデミーでサッカーの技術を磨き、デビューした。その恵まれた身体能力を活かしたスピードと、しなやかで躍動感のあるプレーで知られる。

Leona Lewis
レオナ・ルイス（1985- ）

歌手。ガイアナ系の父親とウェールズ、イタリア、アイルランド系イギリス人の母親の間に、ロンドンで生まれる。イギリスの人気オーディション番組『Xファクター』で優勝してデビューした。2008年の北京オリンピック閉会式では、次回開催地ロンドンを代表して出演した。

Zayn Malik
ゼイン・マリク（1993- ）

イングランドとアイルランド出身の男性5人で結成されたボーイズ・グループ、ワン・ダイレクションのメンバー。パキスタン系イングランド人の父親と、アイルランドの血を引くイングランド人の母親を持つ。

Let's Talk about the UK!
英国コラム①

3人のイギリス民間人が始めたナショナルトラスト運動
Day 3　The Scenery Is Breathtaking, Isn't It? より

　「ナショナルトラスト」とは何でしょうか。ナショナルトラストは、森林や海岸などの自然保護や歴史的建造物の維持を目的とした非営利団体で、その活動を「ナショナルトラスト運動」と言います。正式な名称は「National Trust for Places of Historic Interest or Natural Beauty（歴史的名所や自然的景勝地のためのナショナルトラスト）」です。

　18世紀後半、イギリスでは産業革命が盛んになりました。社会が発展していく一方で、豊かな自然や美しい景観は荒廃していきました。そうした状況を目の当たりにした3人の活動家によって始められたのが、ナショナルトラストです。20世紀以降は、社会の変動によって維持管理が難しくなった貴族やジェントリ（地主層）が昔から所有していた建物や土地などもゆずり受け、保護の対象にしています。ナショナルトラストは、こうした歴史的な建造物などを一般に公開することで、地域社会の観光促進に寄与すると同時に、その入場料などを保全・保護のための活動資金にしています。

　ナショナルトラストの施設入場料は、現在約10ポンド（およそ1700円）です。ナショナルトラストのメンバーになると無料で入場することができます。Day 3でも触れられているヒルトップの他、ビートルズのポール・マッカートニーが幼少期を過ごした家や、詩人でデザイナーのウィリアム・モリスのレッド・ハウスなどもナショナルトラストの保護を受けています。

自分好みの展示がきっと見つかる！ ロンドンの美術館・博物館
Day 4　What Do You Suggest We Do Today? より

　ロンドンには、大英博物館のようにすべての展示品を見るのに何日もかかるような大きなものから、街中にある屋敷ひとつを使って運営されているところまで、多種多様な美術館や博物館があります。Day 4でもたくさんの博物館や美術館が登場しましたので、簡単に説明しましょう。

　トラファルガー広場の北にあるナショナル・ギャラリーには、レオナルド・ダ・ヴィンチから、セザンヌやゴッホといった著名な画家の絵画が揃っています。ヴィクトリア・アンド・アルバート博物館（V＆A）では工芸品やデザインを中心とした豊富なコレクションが展示され、家具やガラス細工、写真、織り物などさまざまな作品を鑑賞することができます。シャーロック・ホームズ博物館は「名探偵ホームズが住んでいた」とされるベイカー・ストリート221番地bにあり、小説の中で描写されているとおりの部屋が再現されています。カートゥーン博物館ではその名の通り、18世紀初期からのイギリスの風刺画やコミックなどのマンガ文化を紹介しています。チョコレート博物館はブリクストンにある2012年にオープンした博物館で、家族で楽しめる展示やイベントが人気です。

　芸術品を維持するだけでもお金が相当かかるのですが、多くの博物館・美術館は入場無料となっています。これは、イギリスにとうとうと流れる〝芸術鑑賞はあらゆる人にとって教育の場である〟という芸術に対する考え方や哲学が、しっかりと根づいているからと言えるでしょう。そのような博物館や美術館に行くと、出入り口近くに募金箱が置いてあることに気付くはずです。目安は5ポンド程度と言われていますが、いくら入れても構いません。またどの国の通貨でもよいのです。旅行中に使い切れなかった硬貨などを入れるのも良いかもしれませんね。

Day 6: What's It Like Being a Student in the UK?

大学生でいるのも楽じゃない！

クリス先生とタケシの2人がやってきたのは、オックスフォード。
ロンドンから西へ約80kmほどの位置にある、ケンブリッジと並ぶ学生の街です。
イギリスでの学生生活に興味を持った様子のタケシですが、
充実した施設での楽しそうなキャンパスライフの一方で、
授業料上昇や学費ローン返済の問題など、
経済的な状況による、厳しい現実もあるようです。

Listen to the Dialogue

DL 28　CD 28

会話文の音声を聞いて、空所に適切な語を書き入れましょう。
完成したら、ペアになって会話の練習をしてみましょう。

Chris: So, this is Oxford – the 'city of dreaming spires' – and home to one of the 1._____ _____ universities in the world.

Takeshi: It's a dream come true to be here. What's it 2._____ _____ a student in the UK, Chris?

Chris: Well, most British students believe that university is not only about broadening your mind, but also about broadening 3._____ _____.

Takeshi: Do you mean British students don't like studying?

Chris: No! Students here study hard, but they also 4._____ _____. They have a vibrant social life.

Takeshi: Sounds cool.

Chris: Every university has a students' union that organises 5._____ _____ of social and sporting events. Most have their own bars and restaurants offering subsidised food and drinks, too.

Takeshi: That's wonderful because students are always 6._____ _____ money, right?

Chris: Absolutely!

Notes home「本拠地」　city of dreaming spires「夢見る尖塔の街」　vibrant「活気のある」
subsidised「補助金を受けた」

▶▶▶51ページのコラムも参照

Expressions for Everyday English

Do you mean (that) ~ ?「～ということですか」

分からないことをハッキリと確認したり、訂正する機会を与えたりするような場合に使う表現です。動詞 mean「～を意味する」を使い「あなたは～ということを意味するのですか」という文章を作ります。通常、mean の後に節（S + V）が続きます。

🎧 DL 29　💿 CD 29

Do you mean (that) you aren't coming with us?　僕らと一緒に行かないということ？
Do you mean you actually had a date with her?　ひょっとして彼女と本当にデートしたの？
Do you mean he passed the final exam?　彼が最終試験に合格したということですか。
Do you mean she won't attend the class?　彼女はその授業に出ないつもりってこと？

Let's Try!

学習した表現を使って自由に英文を作り、ペアになって会話をしてみましょう。

A: Do you mean ＿＿＿＿＿＿＿＿＿＿？ ＿＿＿＿＿＿＿＿＿＿ということですか。
B: Yes, ＿＿＿＿＿＿＿＿＿＿．　ええ、＿＿＿＿＿＿＿＿＿＿。

Useful Vocabulary

🎧 DL 30　💿 CD 30

以下は、次ページで学習するトピックに関する重要語句です。
それぞれの語句の意味に当てはまる日本語を、選択肢から選びましょう。

1. due to　　　　［　］
2. attend　　　　［　］
3. as of　　　　［　］
4. tuition fee　　［　］
5. apply for　　　［　］
6. grant　　　　　［　］
7. encourage　　　［　］
8. scheme　　　　［　］
9. expect　　　　［　］
10. accommodation ［　］

　a. ～現在で　**b.**（当然のこととして）～を期待する　**c.** ～に出席する・通う
　d. ～を奨励する・勧める　**e.** 計画、案　**f.** ～のせいで、～のため
　g. 授業料　**h.** 下宿、アパート　**i.** 奨学金　**j.** ～に申し込む

Reading: Chris's Insight

DL 31, 32   CD 31   CD 32

Study at University - at a Price!

Higher education in Britain used to be free, but this was stopped in 1998 ***due to*** a large increase in the number of young people wanting to ***attend*** university. ***As of*** 2012, universities were allowed to charge up to £9,000 a year in ***tuition fees***. Students can ***apply for*** a government loan that is paid directly to the university or college, and begin repaying the loan when they earn over £21,000 a year. Students can also apply for a loan to help cover living costs. Students from low-income households may also apply for a ***grant*** that they do not have to pay back. On top of that, universities are ***encouraged*** to introduce their own ***schemes*** to enable such students to have a higher education. But no matter how expensive fees are, the majority of British university students do not ***expect*** their parents to fork out the necessary funds; they try their best to pay their fees themselves.

The buildings of Hertford College, Oxford. Two students are seen wearing the academic dress of undergraduates.

One thing that has changed is that more students currently live at home in order to save on ***accommodation*** and food costs. In the past, students learned to be highly independent by living away from home, but now they are in danger of losing out on this valuable experience.

Notes £ = pound パウンド、またはポンド。イギリスの通貨単位（1ポンドは約170円）。 begin repaying「返済を始める」 a year「1年につき」 households「家庭」 on top of that = in addition to that「それに加え」 no matter how...「どんなに～でも」10ページ (Day 1) のNotesも参照。 fork out「（しぶしぶ）～を支払う」 losing out on...「～を見逃す（こと）・逸する（こと）」losingはloseの動名詞。

Reading Comprehension

本文の内容に合わせて、質問の答えとして正しいものを選択肢から選びましょう。

1. What change was made to university education in 1998?
   a. Students no longer had to pay for it
   b. Students had to begin paying for it
   c. More young people wanted it

2. Who can apply for a government loan?
   a. All students
   b. Only students who earn more than £21,000 a year
   c. Only students from low-income families

3. What is a possible disadvantage of students living at home?
   a. They will not save a lot of money
   b. They will not have good food
   c. They will not learn to be independent

Writing Exercises

本章中で使われている表現を参考にして、以下の英文を完成させましょう。

1. そのサッカーチームは主力選手を失いかねない状況です。
   The football team is in _____ _____ losing key players.

2. リバプールに住むのはどんな感じですか。
   What's it _____ _____ in Liverpool?

3. 飛行機のおかげで、私たちは短期間で世界一周ができます。
   Aeroplanes _____ _____ to go around the world in a short time.

4. 彼らは減量するために、甘いものを食べるのを止めました。
   They quit eating sweets in _____ _____ lose weight.

Day 7: Mmm... It Sounds Too Risky

賭けてみる？ ブックメーカーの行く末は

ロンドン市内をめぐるウォーキングツアー中にタケシが見かけたのは、
欧米の民間「賭け事」業者、ブックメーカー。
日本では公営以外のものは違法ですが、イギリスでは免許制の合法。
イギリス人は賭け事が大好きで、大衆文化として生活に浸透しています。
街中にはその店舗も並び、かなり身近な存在ですが、
ここにもインターネットの波が押し寄せているようです。

Listen to the Dialogue

DL 33　CD 33

会話文の音声を聞いて、空所に適切な語を書き入れましょう。
完成したら、ペアになって会話の練習をしてみましょう。

Takeshi: I joined a 1._____ _____ of the West End of London today and saw lots of shops called 'bookmakers', but there were 2._____ _____ in them.

Chris: Ha! Ha! That's because a bookmaker is a place where you can bet on sporting and 3._____ _____.

Takeshi: The British must love gambling because these shops are everywhere.

Chris: That's true. We'll 4._____ _____ almost anything. Betting shops date back some 200 years, and betting is now part and parcel of British life and culture.

Takeshi: And do 5._____ _____ think that's OK?

Chris: Well, it's not everyone's cup of tea, but most people enjoy the 6._____ of the occasional bet.

Takeshi: Mmm... I don't think I'd like to try. It sounds too risky.

Chris: Well, to each their own.

Notes West End「ウエストエンド」ロンドンの行政、商業、文化施設などが集中している地区。　part and parcel「本質的な部分、要点」　everyone's cup of tea「[口語] 皆の好み」　occasional「たまの、時折の」　to each their own「人の好みは様々だ」

Expressions for Everyday English

It sounds ~「～のように聞こえる」「～のように思われる」

sound は「音」という意味の名詞としてだけでなく、動詞としても使われ、人の言動や物事の状態・状況などについて感想や意見を即座に述べることができます。sound の後は形容詞が来ますが、名詞を置く場合は、It sounds like + 名詞（句）の形になります。

🎧 DL 34　💿 CD 34

It sounds great!　それは素晴らしい。
It sounds strange.　それは変だな。
It sounds unlikely.　それはありそうにないな。
It sounds like a wonderful idea!　それは素晴らしい考えだ。[名詞句]

Let's Try!

学習した表現を使って自由に英文を作り、ペアになって会話をしてみましょう。

A: Why don't we _____ this Saturday?　今度の土曜に_____しない？
B: _____！　それは_____だね！

Useful Vocabulary

🎧 DL 35　💿 CD 35

以下は、次ページで学習するトピックに関する重要語句です。
それぞれの語句の意味に当てはまる日本語を、選択肢から選びましょう。

1. ban　　　　　　[　　]　　6. ruin　　　　　　[　　]
2. hold back　　　[　　]　　7. competition　　[　　]
3. thirst　　　　　[　　]　　8. profitable　　　[　　]
4. legal　　　　　[　　]　　9. thereby　　　　[　　]
5. acceptable　　[　　]　　10. landscape　　[　　]

> **a.** ～を抑える　**b.** 合法的な　**c.** ～を破滅させる　**d.** 風景
> **e.** ～を禁止する　**f.** その結果　**g.** 強い欲望、渇望　**h.** 競争
> **i.** 儲かる　**j.** 受け入れられる

Day 7　Mmm... It Sounds Too Risky

Reading: Chris's Insight

Betting Shops on Every High Street

The first betting shops appeared in London in 1815 but were then **banned** in 1853. However, nothing can **hold back** the British punter's **thirst** for gambling, so the shops were made **legal** again in 1961. Gambling is not only legal, but is also seen as a socially **acceptable** activity. Betting shops are found on nearly every high street, and Brits will bet, or 'have a flutter', on practically anything: horse racing, football, the gender and names of royal babies, and even the weather!

Betting odds given by a bookmaker, Ladbrokes, for the future Prime Minister during the 2010 UK General Election outside Parliament in Westminster

The positive side of betting is that it brings the government billions of pounds in taxes and creates thousands of jobs. On the negative side, though, it can become a kind of addiction and has **ruined** many lives, especially among poorer people.

Today, betting shops are facing tough **competition** from online gambling, which has become one of the most popular and **profitable** Internet industries. The shops have fought back by upgrading their levels of cleanliness and comfort and by introducing slot machines, **thereby** turning themselves into mini-casinos. But can they survive in this cyber age?

Well, if you put your money on betting shops disappearing from the British **landscape** any time soon, you will almost certainly lose your bet!

Notes betting shops「ブックメーカー、賭け屋」 punter「賭けをする人」 high street「本通り、大通り」
flutter「ちょっとした賭け」 addiction「熱中、中毒」 fought back「巻き返しに出た」foughtはfightの過去形。
cleanliness [発音注意]「清潔さ」cleanの名詞

Reading Comprehension

本文の内容に合わせて、質問の答えとして正しいものを選択肢から選びましょう。

1. How is gambling viewed in Britain?
   a. As a normal human activity
   b. Only as a legal activity
   c. The same as horses and the weather

2. What is one benefit of betting?
   a. People don't have to pay a lot of taxes
   b. It boosts the economy
   c. It can be addictive

3. What is threatening the future of betting shops?
   a. The arrival of online gambling
   b. The arrival of profitable industries
   c. The arrival of mini-casinos

Writing Exercises

本章中で使われている表現を参考にして、以下の英文を完成させましょう。

1. ジュリアは夢を実現しました。
   Julia _____ her dream _____ reality.

2. あのサインを書いている人は、有名に違いありません。
   The person signing autographs _____ _____ famous.

3. その研究グループは、砂漠化を抑えるために植樹を行っています。
   The research group has planted trees to _____ _____ desertification.

4. 私が子供の頃住んでいた家は、とても小さかったです。
   The house _____ I lived when I was a child _____ very small.

Day 8

You Should Try Fish and Chips!

多彩で美味しい！ イギリス料理

イギリスは食事がいまひとつ、なんて昔の話。
今では日本食も含め、さまざまな国の料理を手軽に楽しむことができます。
ジェイミー・オリバーなど人気シェフたちの存在も手伝って、
イギリスの食卓は、健康的でバラエティに富んだものに。
それでも、伝統的なイギリス料理も健在。
今日のディナー、クリス先生とタケシは何を食べる？

Listen to the Dialogue

DL 40　CD 40

会話文の音声を聞いて、空所に適切な語を書き入れましょう。
完成したら、ペアになって会話の練習をしてみましょう。

Chris: Today, I thought we could try some traditional British food.
Takeshi: Really? But ¹＿＿＿＿＿ ＿＿＿＿＿ me it's awful.
Chris: Ha! Ha! Yes, British food has a pretty awful reputation, but times have changed, and so has the ²＿＿＿＿＿ and variety of our food.
Takeshi: So, what can I expect ³＿＿＿＿＿ ＿＿＿＿＿?
Chris: Well, the good news is you can eat food from all over the world – Indian, Chinese, Italian, Thai... You can even find sushi and sashimi!
Takeshi: But that's not what I'd call traditional British food.
Chris: You're right. So, you should try dishes ⁴＿＿＿＿＿ fish and chips, shepherd's pie, roast beef and Yorkshire pudding – they're ⁵＿＿＿＿＿ ＿＿＿＿＿.
Takeshi: Mmm... Now I'm getting hungry. What are we ⁶＿＿＿＿＿ ＿＿＿＿＿?
Chris: OK. Follow me!

Notes reputation「評判」　shepherd's pie「シェパーズ・パイ」羊肉や牛肉とマッシュポテトのパイ。Yorkshire pudding「ヨークシャー・プディング」肉料理に付け合わせられるシュークリームの皮のようなもの。

Expressions for Everyday English

You should ＋動詞の原形「～すべきです」「～すればいいのに」

相手に助言を与えたり、何かを勧める表現です。助動詞 should の後は動詞の原形を置きます。強い命令口調として受け取られることもあり、冒頭に Maybe を付けると「～する方が良いかもしれませんね」と柔らかい表現にすることができます。

🎧 DL 41　💿 CD 41

You should try harder.　あなたはもっと頑張るべきですよ。
You should be more aggressive.　君はもっと積極的になればいいのに。
You should try a different approach.　別の方法を試してみるべきだわ。
Maybe you should go home early.　あなたは早く家に帰るほうがいいわね。

Let's Try!
学習した表現を使って自由に英文を作り、ペアになって会話をしてみましょう。
A: You should _____. _____するべきだよ。
B: OK, I will.　分かった、そうするよ。

Useful Vocabulary

🎧 DL 42　💿 CD 42

以下は、次ページで学習するトピックに関する重要語句です。
それぞれの語句の意味に当てはまる日本語を、選択肢から選びましょう。

1. survey　　　　　　[　　] 　6. serve　　　　　　　[　　]
2. dramatically　　　[　　] 　7. be conscious of　　[　　]
3. varied　　　　　　[　　] 　8. raise　　　　　　　[　　]
4. abroad　　　　　　[　　] 　9. replace　　　　　　[　　]
5. be exposed to　　[　　] 　10. no longer　　　　　[　　]

> **a.** もはや～でない　**b.** 海外へ　**c.**（食事など）を出す　**d.** 調査
> **e.** ～に取って代わる　**f.** 劇的に　**g.** ～を高める　**h.** ～を意識する
> **i.** ～に触れる　**j.** 変化に富んだ

Day 8　You Should Try Fish and Chips!

Reading: Chris's Insight

DL 43 ~ 45　CD 43 ~ CD 45

Yummy! Exotic and Healthy British Food

What is the most popular British dish? Fish and chips? No! According to a recent **survey**, the correct answer is chicken tikka masala, a spicy Indian curry. A well-known Member of Parliament even called it 'a true British national dish'. The point is that the British people's tastes have changed **dramatically** over the last 40 years or so, and British food culture has become far more **varied** and exotic. Why? Well, more and more Brits go **abroad** for their holidays and **are exposed to** all kinds of different foods. Also, Britain is a much more multicultural society than before, so you can find restaurants **serving** food from every corner of the world.

Chicken tikka masala

British food has also become healthier as many people **are** now far more **conscious of** what they eat. Popular TV cooking shows with celebrity chefs like Jamie Oliver and Gordon Ramsay have helped **raise** people's awareness about the importance of healthy eating. Jamie Oliver also led a campaign to improve the quality of school dinners throughout Britain, **replacing** junk food with more nourishing options.

British food had a reputation for being boring, tasteless, and unhealthy, but this is definitely **no longer** the case. Try it and see!

Notes　chicken tikka masala「チキン・ティッカ・マサラ」イギリス生まれのインド料理。　**Member of Parliament**「下院議員」　exotic「異国情緒豊かな」　multicultural「多文化的な」　celebrity chefs「有名人シェフ」　Jamie Oliver　ジェイミー・オリバー（1975- ）。イングランドの料理人。　**Gordon Ramsay**　ゴードン・ラムゼイ（1968- ）。スコットランドの料理人。　awareness「知ること、気づくこと」　nourishing「栄養価の高い」　case「実情」

▶▶ 50ページの『本書に登場する人名・団体名』も参照

Reading Comprehension

本文の内容に合わせて、質問の答えとして正しいものを選択肢から選びましょう。

1. What is chicken tikka masala?
    a. The favourite food of a Member of Parliament
    b. The most popular food in Britain
    c. The topic of a recent survey

2. Why has the Brits' taste in food changed?
    a. Because they enjoy going on holiday
    b. Because they like to eat out a lot
    c. Because they live in a multicultural society

3. What has helped to make British food healthier?
    a. The replacement of junk food
    b. TV cooking programmes
    c. School dinners

Writing Exercises

本章中で使われている表現を参考にして、以下の英文を完成させましょう。

1. 以前に比べ自信がつきました。
   I feel _____ confident than _____.

2. 消防士はしばしば大きな危険にさらされています。
   Firefighters _____ often _____ to great danger.

3. 宇宙への旅行はもはや途方もない夢ではありません。
   A trip to space is _____ _____ just a fantastic _____.

4. これはまさに、私がずっと欲しいと思っていたものです。
   This is exactly _____ I have always wanted.

Day 9 It's Fun Listening to Different Accents

8月のエディンバラ

イギリス本島の北部に位置するスコットランド。
早速その独特なアクセントに触れ、
この国の多様性を実感した様子のタケシです。
スコットランドはキルトやバグパイプ、スコッチウィスキーなどで有名ですが、
8月に開かれるエディンバラ・フェスティバルは、世界中の人たちが訪れる、
一度は目にしておきたい芸術の祭典です。

Listen to the Dialogue

DL 46　CD 46

会話文の音声を聞いて、空所に適切な語を書き入れましょう。
完成したら、ペアになって会話の練習をしてみましょう。

Takeshi: I couldn't understand much of what the taxi driver was saying.
Chris: Welcome to Scotland, Takeshi! The Scottish accent can be 1._____ _____.
Takeshi: Everywhere we've visited, the people speak differently.
Chris: Yes, that's one special feature of British English. 2._____ _____ national accents like Scottish, Irish, and Welsh, 3._____ _____ has its own distinctive local one.
Takeshi: That makes it a bit more difficult 4._____ _____ of English, but I like all these regional differences. It's fun listening to them.
Chris: I'm glad to hear that. Now, we have to choose what events we want to go to here at the Edinburgh 5._____.
Takeshi: May I make a request, Chris?
Chris: Of course.
Takeshi: I'd love to see the Royal Edinburgh Military Tattoo.
Chris: OK. Let's see if we can get 6._____ _____ online.

Notes feature「特徴」　distinctive「独特の」　one 'accent'を受ける代名詞　regional「地域の」
the Royal Edinburgh Military Tattoo「ロイヤル・エディンバラ・ミリタリー・タトゥー」エディンバラ城でスコットランド軍楽隊と兵士が出し物をするパレード。tattooは軍隊の帰営ラッパのこと。

Expressions for Everyday English

May I＋動詞の原形?「～してよろしいでしょうか」

助動詞 may を使って、話者が相手に何らかの動作の許可を求める丁寧な表現です。目上の人に May I ~ ? と聞き、相手が Yes, you may. と答えると、「ええどうぞ」と許可を与えることになります。友達などには Sure や Certainly と答えます。

🎧 DL 47　💿 CD 47

May I ask you a favour?　ひとつお願いしてもよろしいでしょうか。
May I speak to Mary?　[電話で] メアリーさんをお願します。
May I borrow your mobile phone?　携帯を貸してもらえますか。
May I make a proposal?　提案をしてよろしいでしょうか。

Let's Try!
学習した表現を使って自由に英文を作り、ペアになって会話をしてみましょう。
A: May I _____ ? _____ してよろしいですか。
B: No. I'm sorry, you can't.　ご遠慮いただけますか。

Useful Vocabulary

🎧 DL 48　💿 CD 48

以下は、次ページで学習するトピックに関する重要語句です。
それぞれの語句の意味に当てはまる日本語を、選択肢から選びましょう。

1. leading　　　　[　]
2. globe　　　　　[　]
3. assured　　　　[　]
4. highlight　　　[　]
5. hold　　　　　 [　]
6. magnificent　　　　　[　]
7. turn off　　　　　　 [　]
8. apparently　　　　　[　]
9. ceremonial　　　　　[　]
10. catch a glimpse of　[　]

> **a.** 儀式の　**b.** 壮大な　**c.** 呼び物　**d.** 地球、世界　**e.** 約束された
> **f.** ～をちらっと見る　**g.** ～を開催する　**h.** どうやら～らしい
> **i.** ～を閉める・止める　**j.** 有数の、優れた

Day 9　It's Fun Listening to Different Accents

Reading: Chris's Insight

An Unforgettable Cultural Experience in Edinburgh

Edinburgh is one of the world's **leading** festival cities, holding 12 different festivals a year. Artists come from every corner of the **globe** and perform all over the city, both in theatres and on the streets. Visitors are **assured** of an unforgettable cultural experience. August is the most action-packed month, and one of the **highlights** is the Royal Edinburgh Military Tattoo. This performance by military bands, with drums and bagpipes, is **held** in the **magnificent** grounds of Edinburgh Castle. The show attracts over 200,000 people every year.

Scottish Pipes exhibition at Edinburgh Military Tattoo

The word 'tattoo' has an interesting history. It comes from the Dutch words 'tap toe', meaning '**turn off** the tap'. **Apparently**, British army bands in Belgium in the 18th century used to play the drums and pipes each night as a signal for pubs to turn off the beer taps. Then soldiers would have to stop drinking and return to their barracks. 'Tattoo' later came to mean any kind of **ceremonial** performance by army bands.

If you visit Edinburgh, you should make time for a trip to the beautiful Scottish Highlands. Loch Lomond and Loch Ness are not so far, and if you're lucky, you may even **catch a glimpse of** 'Nessie' – the famous Loch Ness monster!

Notes a year「1年につき」 action-packed「アクション満載の、活動的な」 military bands「軍楽隊」 Dutch「オランダ語の」 tap「(樽などの)栓、蛇口」 Belgium「ベルギー」実際にイギリス軍が駐留していたのは、現在のベルギーを含む当時はthe Low Countriesと呼ばれていた地域。 pipes = bagpipes「バグパイプ」 barracks「兵舎」 make time「時間をとる」 Loch Lomond「ローモンド湖」 Loch Ness「ネス湖」

▶▶ 6ページも参照

Reading Comprehension

本文の内容に合わせて、質問の答えとして正しいものを選択肢から選びましょう。

1. Where are Edinburgh festival performances held?
   a. On every corner of the globe
   b. In every part of the city
   c. Only in theatres

2. What is the Royal Edinburgh Military Tattoo?
   a. A display by military bands
   b. A musical show played every night in pubs
   c. A type of army band performance that started in Holland

3. What can you see not far from Edinburgh?
   a. The Loch Ness monster
   b. More festival activities
   c. The Scottish Highlands

Writing Exercises

本章中で使われている表現を参考にして、以下の英文を完成させましょう。

1. お医者さんがたくさん食べるのを止めるよう言いました。
   My doctor told me to ＿＿＿＿＿＿ ＿＿＿＿＿＿ so much.

2. あなたの結婚式はどこでやるの？
   Where ＿＿＿＿＿＿ your wedding ceremony be ＿＿＿＿＿＿?

3. 雨が止むのを待ちましょう。
   Let's wait ＿＿＿＿＿＿ the rain ＿＿＿＿＿＿ stop.

4. モーリスは私に、フランス語を話せるかどうか尋ねました。
   Maurice ＿＿＿＿＿＿ me ＿＿＿＿＿＿ I could speak French.

Day 10

Do You Fancy Something Sweet?

そのチョコレート、原料はどこから？

甘いものが大好きなイギリス人。
スーパーマーケットのお菓子売り場に行けば、
キャドバリー社などのチョコレート製品がたくさん並んでいます。
チョコレートの原料カカオは、多くが発展途上国産。
今イギリスでは、途上国の生産者や労働者たちとの公正な取引、
「フェアトレード」が注目されています。

Listen to the Dialogue

DL 52　CD 52

会話文の音声を聞いて、空所に適切な語を書き入れましょう。
完成したら、ペアになって会話の練習をしてみましょう。

Chris: Let's ¹._____ _____ the supermarket to find something for our lunch today.

Takeshi: OK. Hmm… these sandwiches look good, don't you think?

Chris: Yeah. We could get a ²._____ _____ as well.

Takeshi: Good idea.

Chris: Do you fancy ³._____ _____, too?

Takeshi: Yes, I do. Wow! I can't believe how many kinds of sweets and chocolate there are. The ⁴._____ are endless!

Chris: Welcome to the UK! We just love sweet things. Oh, look at the queues at the tills.

Takeshi: Never mind. Hey, they even have chocolate and sweets by the checkouts.

Chris: That's right. But lots of people are ⁵._____ _____ _____ this because they say it contributes to obesity.

Takeshi: I read that about 25% of kids in Britain are ⁶._____.

Chris: I'm afraid it's true.

Notes queues「行列」　tills = checkouts「レジ」　contribute to…「〜の一因となる」　obesity「肥満」

Expressions for Everyday English

I'm afraid (that) ~「あいにく~だと思います」「残念ながら~です」

良くないことや相手に対し不作法になることを伝える際に、内容を和らげたり、遠慮がちに尋ねたりする場合に用いられる表現です。afraid の後に節（S + V）が続き、話者や相手に望ましくない内容が置かれます。

🎧 DL 53   💿 CD 53

I'm afraid it will rain tomorrow.　どうやら、明日は雨のようです。
I'm afraid you'll have to rewrite this report.
　　　　　　　　君はこのレポートを書き直さなければならないと思いますよ。
I'm afraid I don't eat meat.　すみませんが、私は肉を食べません。
I'm afraid he's not available right now.　あいにく、彼は今手が離せません。

Let's Try!

学習した表現を使って自由に英文を作り、ペアになって会話をしてみましょう。

A: Will we have a ＿＿＿＿＿＿＿ tomorrow?　明日＿＿＿＿＿＿＿があるかな？
B: ＿＿＿＿＿＿＿＿＿＿＿＿＿＿＿＿＿＿.　＿＿＿＿＿＿＿＿＿＿＿＿＿＿＿＿＿＿。

Useful Vocabulary

🎧 DL 54   💿 CD 54

以下は、次ページで学習するトピックに関する重要語句です。
それぞれの語句の意味に当てはまる日本語を、選択肢から選びましょう。

1. regularly　　　[　　]
2. billion　　　　[　　]
3. wealthy　　　　[　　]
4. widespread　　[　　]
5. nation　　　　[　　]
6. found　　　　　[　　]
7. promote　　　　[　　]
8. ingredient　　[　　]
9. committed to　[　　]
10. look out for　[　　]

a. 国、国家　**b.** 普及して　**c.** 原料、材料　**d.** 10 億
e. ~を振興する　**f.** ~を設立する　**g.** ~に熱心で・尽力して
h. 普段から　**i.** 裕福な　**j.** ~を探し出す

Day 10　Do You Fancy Something Sweet?

Reading: Chris's Insight

A Sweet Tooth - Fair Trade Chocolate Tastes Sweeter

The British are famous for their love of sweets. According to a 2012 survey, 84% of adults eat sweets **regularly**, and over three **billion** pounds are spent on sweets every year. Brits certainly have a 'sweet tooth'! This love of sweets goes back hundreds of years, especially among the more **wealthy** people.
5 It became more **widespread** as the price of sugar went down in the 19th century. Chocolate is an incredibly popular sweet. We could say Britain is a **nation** of chocoholics! And when it comes to chocolate, Cadbury, the world-famous UK chocolate maker, is king. This company, **founded** nearly 200 years ago, can rightly be considered a part of British culture.

10 The UK is a world leader in **promoting** fair trade, and Cadbury has begun to support this important movement. It is now using fair trade **ingredients** in some of
15 its chocolate and is **committed to** expanding this use in the future. As a result, the living conditions of poor cocoa farmers should greatly improve. The next time you buy
20 chocolate, **look out for** the FAIRTRADE label. You, too, can make a difference, and the chocolate will taste so much sweeter.

Farm workers in Ghana spreading cocoa beans to dry in the sun.

Notes have a 'sweet tooth'「甘いものが好きである」 incredibly「信じられないほど、非常に」 chocoholic チョコレートが異常に好きな人のこと。cf. alcoholic when it comes to...「〜のことになると」 Cadbury キャドバリー。イギリスの菓子・飲料メーカー。 rightly「当然、然るべく」 fair trade「フェアトレード」公正な取引、またそれを実現させるための運動を指す。 make a difference「変化をもたらす、(状況を)改善する」

▶▶ 50ページの『本書に登場する人名・団体名』、および51ページのコラムも参照

Reading Comprehension

本文の内容に合わせて、質問の答えとして正しいものを選択肢から選びましょう。

1. Why did sweets become popular among all British people in the 19th century?
   a. Because the price of sugar dropped
   b. Because wealthy people loved sweets
   c. Because billions of pounds were spent on sweets

2. What is Cadbury?
   a. A chocolate company that is popular among kings
   b. A chocolate company that considers British culture
   c. A chocolate company that is known worldwide

3. How does Cadbury help the fair trade movement?
   a. It leads the world in fair trade
   b. Some of its products use fair trade ingredients
   c. It produces sweeter-tasting chocolate

Writing Exercises

本章中で使われている表現を参考にして、以下の英文を完成させましょう。

1. そのショッピングセンターは、地域社会に大きな変化をもたらしました。
   The shopping centre _____ a big _____ to the local community.

2. このネクタイ、僕に似合うかな？
   _____ this tie _____ good on me?

3. その少年は何か温かい飲み物を欲しがりました。
   The little boy wanted _____ _____ to drink.

4. 彼は英語を話しますが、ロシア語も話します。
   He speaks English, and Russian _____ _____ .

Day 10　Do You Fancy Something Sweet?

Names of People & Groups

本書に登場する人名・団体名②

Day 8
Jamie Oliver
ジェイミー・オリバー（1975- ）

BBC放送の料理番組『裸のシェフ』Naked Chefで人気を博した料理人。イギリス料理は不味い、というイメージを変えたと言われ、レシピ本も多く出版されている。近年は、公立校の給食を健康的なメニューにするなど、子どもたちの食に対する意識を改善する活動に取り組んでいる。

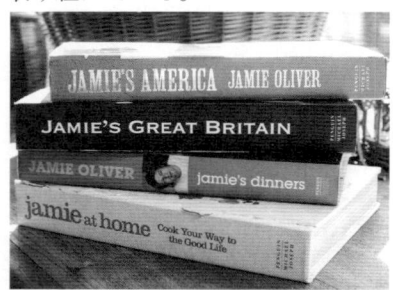

Gordon Ramsay
ゴードン・ラムゼイ（1968- ）

スコットランドの料理人。サッカー選手を目指すもケガのため断念し、シェフに転身。オーナーを務める店はミシュランの星をいくつも獲得している。短気で毒舌なキャラクターが受け、リアリティ番組などでも活躍するセレブリティ・シェフである。

Day 10
Cadbury
キャドバリー　菓子・飲料ブランド

19世紀始めに、ジョン・キャドバリーがバーミンガムで開業した食料品店から始まった菓子・飲料の老舗ブランド。1905年に発売したDairy Milk Chocolateは、イギリスで一番人気があるチョコレートとも言われ、現在の板チョコの基盤となったとされている。バーミンガムに「キャドバリー・ワールド」というチョコレートをテーマにした観光施設がある。

Day 13
Vivienne Westwood
ヴィヴィアン・ウエストウッド（1941- ）

ファッションデザイナー、ファッションブランドの名称。反逆性とエレガンスを兼ね備えたアバンギャルドなデザインで知られるが、ウエストウッド本人は、大英帝国勲章の中でも高位の勲位を受勲した女性に対してのみ使用される「デイム」の敬称を持つ。

Burberry
バーバリー　老舗服飾メーカー

トマス・バーバリーによって1856年創立された。第一次大戦のイギリス陸軍のために作った機能的なコートが元になったトレンチコートで有名。コートの裏地に使われた「バーバリー・チェック」はブランドの権威を一気に高めたと言われる。数々の政治家や俳優など著名人に愛された。

Paul Smith
ポール・スミス（1964- ）

ファッションデザイナー、ファッションブランドの名称。ブランドのシンボルにもなっている色鮮やかなストライプ柄など遊び心のあるデザインが人気。イギリスの伝統的な技術にモダンな価値を融合させたブランドと言われている。

Let's Talk about the UK!
英国コラム②

イギリスの大学での勉強やキャンパスライフ、日本との違い
Day 6　What's It Like Being a Student in the UK? より

　大学で学士号を取得する場合、日本では4年制が普通ですが、イギリスの大学では、通常のフルタイムのコースで、1年目からすぐに専門課程へと入り3年で全課程を修了します（コースによっては4年の場合もあります）。日本の大学で主流となっている講義形式の授業も行われますがそれは一部で、講義内容を補うために行われるセミナーや、教授もしくはチューターとのマンツーマン、あるいは2、3名で行われる個別指導のチュートリアル制で勉強します。

　イギリスの多くの大学はいわゆる国公立大学で、政府によってその教育水準・研究水準が決められ、管理されています。そのため学生は能動的に取り組むことが求められ、「教えてもらう」よりも自分の考えをしっかりと構築し、それを人に分かってもらえるよう工夫し発言できる力を養成する必要があります。1年生の時から課題の量や読むべき本の数も、日本の学生に比べ段違いに多いです。

　学業だけでなく、生活の面でも日本とイギリスの大学には違いがあります。クリス先生もタケシに説明しているように、ほとんどの大学には学生組合（Students' Union）があり、キャンパスライフの中心的存在となっています。利用料金は非常に安く、座って話せるスペースやスーパーマーケット、バー、食事ができる場所、あるいは銀行や書店、それに美容室や理髪店なども入っていて生活には困りません。音楽イベントやパーティなど、勉強時間以外の時間を充実させるための催しも多数用意されています。また、アルバイト関連や、クラブの勧誘・メンバー募集などたくさんの情報が載っている掲示板もあります。これらの学生組合は、卒業生や在校生によって運営されています。

キャドバリーも取り組むフェアトレードって？
Day 10　Do You Fancy Something Sweet? より

　最近日本でも見かけるようになった「フェアトレード」という言葉やその関連商品、これらは一体何でしょうか。普段、私たちが手にする製品の中には、発展途上国で生産された原料や製品が使われ、驚くほどに安価で取引が行われているものや、正当な賃金が生産者に支払われていないものが含まれている場合があります。「フェアトレード（fair trade）」は「公平な取引」という意味で、こうした状況を是正しようという取り組みのことを「フェアトレード」と呼んでいます。

　例えばコーヒー豆や、イギリス人が大好きなチョコレート製品。これらの商品の原料は南米やアフリカ、アジアの途上国で産出されているものが多く、他の輸入品に比べ非常に安く取引されています。「公平な取引」、つまり適正な料金や賃金の支払いと継続的な買い取りを通じて、こうした立場の弱い途上国の生産者や労働者の生活を改善・安定させ、自立させることを目指しているのです。

　コーヒーやチョコレート以外にも、バナナなどの果物や香辛料、コットン、シードオイルなどがフェアトレード商品に含まれています。このような商品を購入する際、誰が作っているのかを気にしてみましょう。フェアトレード運動はヨーロッパ諸国を中心に1960年代から本格的に広まりました。イギリスで最も人気のあるチョコレートバーのひとつ、キャドバリーのDairy Milk Chocolateなどにも、フェアトレード商品が見られます。日本で始まったのは1990年代でまだまだ市場は小さいと言えます。最近では、イオンや無印良品などの大手企業も積極的に活動に取り組んでいるようです。

Day 11: I Guess I Should Have a Black-Cab Experience

市内どこへも最短距離で！ロンドンタクシー

これからタクシーに乗ってどこかへ向かう様子の、クリス先生とタケシ。
名物の赤い2階建てバス、ダブルデッカーと並んで
黒い車体のタクシーは、ロンドンの風景の一部となっています。
世界一難しいと言われる試験に合格した、誇り高きブラック・キャブの運転手。
ロンドン中の道という道がインプットされたその頭脳を駆使して、
一番のルートで目的地に送り届けてくれます。

Listen to the Dialogue

DL 57　CD 57

会話文の音声を聞いて、空所に適切な語を書き入れましょう。
完成したら、ペアになって会話の練習をしてみましょう。

Takeshi: 1._____ _____ we going to your friend's house, Chris?

Chris: Let's take a black cab. It'll be faster because my friend 2._____ _____ near a tube station or bus stop.

Takeshi: Er... sorry, but what's a 'black cab'?

Chris: Oh, traditional London taxis are known as black cabs.

Takeshi: But they're 3._____ _____ black!

Chris: Ha! Ha! That's true, Takeshi. They come in a 4._____ _____ colours nowadays. But they all 5._____ _____ be black. I think they're as much a part of British culture as the Tower of London or even cricket!

Takeshi: Well, I guess I should definitely have a black-cab experience, then.

Chris: 6._____ _____, so let's go. Taxi! Taxi!

Notes　black cab「ブラック・キャブ」ロンドンのタクシーの別称。　tube station「地下鉄の駅」　the Tower of London「ロンドン塔」中世の城塞で、現在でも式典などで使われる武器などの保管庫として使用されている。　cricket「クリケット」主にイギリス文化圏で人気の、野球の原型と言われる古くからあるスポーツ。

Expressions for Everyday English

I guess (that) ~「~と推測します」「~じゃないかな」「~と思う」

確たる証拠がなかったり、話すことをためらう気持ちがあったりするけれども「~と思う」、という時に使います。動詞 guess の後は節（S + V）が来ます。似た表現に、I think ~「（頭で考えて）思う」、I suppose ~「（仮定して）思う」などがあります。

🎧 DL 58 💿 CD 58

I guess that the teacher is around forty.　その先生は 40 歳前後だと思うよ。

I guess it's going to rain.　たぶん雨になるんじゃないかな。

I can't guess at all what you're going to do next.
　　　　　　次に君がどうするつもりなのか、まったく見当がつかないよ。

I guess I'm not hungry any more.　もうお腹いっぱいみたいだ。

Let's Try!

学習した表現を使って自由に英文を作り、ペアになって会話をしてみましょう。

A: I guess _____. _____じゃないかな。

B: Yes, probably.　うん、たぶんね。

Useful Vocabulary

🎧 DL 59 💿 CD 59

以下は、次ページで学習するトピックに関する重要語句です。
それぞれの語句の意味に当てはまる日本語を、選択肢から選びましょう。

1. practically　　[　]
2. these days　　[　]
3. no doubt　　[　]
4. rely on　　[　]
5. inbuilt　　[　]
6. remain　　[　]
7. demanding　　[　]
8. roughly　　[　]
9. landmark　　[　]
10. talkative　　[　]

> **a.** 史跡、目印となるもの　**b.** おそらく　**c.** 作りつけの　**d.** 努力が必要な
> **e.** ~を頼りにする・あてにする　**f.** 最近、近頃　**g.** 実際には
> **h.** おおよそ、概略で　**i.** おしゃべり好きの　**j.** ~のままである

Reading: Chris's Insight

The Knowledge - A Satnav in the Brain

Practically everyone uses a satellite navigation system, or satnav, in their car to find their way around ***these days***, right? Wrong! If you are in London and take one of the famous 'black cabs', as the taxis are affectionately called, you will ***no doubt*** be surprised to see that the drivers do not ***rely on*** electronic satnavs. Rather, they have an '***inbuilt*** satnav' in their brains! This is because anyone wishing to become a London cabbie has to take what is called 'The Knowledge'. Started in 1865, this examination ***remains*** one of the most ***demanding*** in the world, testing the driver's in-depth knowledge of the ***roughly*** 25,000 streets and 20,000 ***landmarks*** in London. It's so tough that most people need to take the test more than ten times over a period of nearly three years before finally passing.

The good news for the passenger, though, is that no matter how bad the traffic, the London cabbie will always get you to your destination by the shortest and quickest possible route. On top of that, visitors from overseas can also practise their English, as London cabbies are among the most ***talkative*** and friendly taxi drivers in the world!

Black London taxi on a bridge in front of Big Ben and the Houses of Parliament

Notes satellite navigation system (satnav)「衛星測位システム」複数の衛星から送信される信号を受信し、地表・海上・空中で自らの位置を知ることができるシステム。日本ではカーナビゲーションシステムと呼ばれることが多い。 affectionately「親しみをこめて」 cabbie「タクシー運転手」 what is called「いわゆる」関係代名詞whatを使った慣用表現。 in-depth「徹底的な」

▶▶ 73ページのコラムも参照

Reading Comprehension

本文の内容に合わせて、質問の答えとして正しいものを選択肢から選びましょう。

1. What do London taxi drivers use to find their way around the city?
   a. An electronic satellite navigation system
   b. A 'black cab'
   c. A kind of navigation system in their brain

2. What is 'The Knowledge'?
   a. A test you have to take over ten times
   b. A test of a driver's detailed knowledge of London
   c. A test that took nearly three years to make

3. What will London cabbies always do?
   a. Get passengers to where they want to go as quickly as possible
   b. Give passengers good news when the traffic is bad
   c. Teach overseas passengers English

Writing Exercises

本章中で使われている表現を参考にして、以下の英文を完成させましょう。

1. 私はそれを聞いて本当にびっくりしましたが、うれしかったです。
   I was really _____ _____ hear that, but I was glad.

2. 紅茶には、コーヒーと同じくらいカフェインがありますか。
   Does tea contain as _____ caffeine _____ coffee?

3. どんなに忙しくても、先生方はいつも私に時間を割いてくれます
   _____ matter _____ busy they are, my teachers _____ make time for me.

4. 君のテストの点、悪いね。しっかり勉強しないからだよ。
   Your test score is bad. _____ is _____ you don't study hard enough.

Day 12: I'm Looking forward to Seeing Wales!

ウェールズ語とチャールズ皇太子

イギリス本島の南西に位置するウェールズ。
英語とは別に世界で最も古い言語とも言われるウェールズ語も公用語として使われ、
また、世界遺産に登録されたたくさんの城郭や、
森林や湖、丘陵、海岸などの豊かな自然を抱えます。
「プリンス・オブ・ウェールズ」の称号をもつチャールズ皇太子と、
その称号が使われるようになった歴史的背景にも注目してみましょう。

Listen to the Dialogue

DL 62　CD 62

会話文の音声を聞いて、空所に適切な語を書き入れましょう。
完成したら、ペアになって会話の練習をしてみましょう。

Chris: You see, just a three-hour drive from London and here we are. Welcome to Cardiff, the 1.＿＿＿＿＿ of Wales!

Takeshi: Thanks! I've been looking forward to seeing another interesting 2.＿＿＿＿＿ ＿＿＿＿＿ the UK.

Chris: And you'll enjoy the sing-song Welsh accent.

Takeshi: There's a Welsh language, too, isn't there?

Chris: Yes, it's 3.＿＿＿＿＿ ＿＿＿＿＿ roughly 20% of the population. It was recognised as an official language in 2011, and it's a compulsory subject in Welsh schools for pupils up to the age of 16.

Takeshi: It's wonderful to keep minority languages 4.＿＿＿＿＿ like that.

Chris: I agree. Now, 5.＿＿＿＿＿ ＿＿＿＿＿, we'll drive up to North Wales and see some of the famous castles.

Takeshi: Great. By the way, Chris, is it okay if 6.＿＿＿＿＿ ＿＿＿＿＿?

Chris: No way, Takeshi! You're not insured!

Notes Cardiff「カーディフ」ウェールズの首都。　official language「公用語」　compulsory subject「必須科目」　up to...「〜まで」　minority「少数の、少数民族の」

Expressions for Everyday English

Is it okay / OK / alright if ~「~してもいいですか」

if 以下のことをしても良いか、と許可や容認をもらうための表現です。it（仮主語）の内容は if + S + V で具体的に示します。親しい間柄の人に対して使えるフレーズです。

DL 63　CD 63

Is it okay if I come in?　入ってもいいですか。

Is it okay if I skip today's club activity?　今日の部活休んでもいいかな？

Is it okay if I open the window?　窓を開けてもいいですか。

Is it okay if I bring my girlfriend to the party?　彼女をパーティに連れて行ってもいい？

Let's Try!

学習した表現を使って自由に英文を作り、ペアになって会話をしてみましょう。

A: Is it okay if _____?　_____ してもいいですか。

B: Of course you will.　もちろん、いいよ。

Useful Vocabulary

DL 64　CD 64

以下は、次ページで学習するトピックに関する重要語句です。
それぞれの語句の意味に当てはまる日本語を、選択肢から選びましょう。

1. outstanding　[　]
2. gorgeous　[　]
3. treasure　[　]
4. invest　[　]
5. heir　[　]
6. throne　[　]
7. title　[　]
8. award　[　]
9. current　[　]
10. pronounce　[　]

> a. 現在の　b. すばらしい　c. 称号　d. 見事な、抜群の
> e. ~を発音する　f. ~を与える　g. 継承者　h. ~を授ける
> i. 宝　j. 王位

Day 12　I'm Looking forward to Seeing Wales!

Reading: Chris's Insight

A World Heritage Site and the Prince of Wales

Wales is a country of **outstanding** natural beauty: Snowdonia National Park with the highest mountain in England and Wales; the Gower peninsula with the best beach in the UK; and the **gorgeous** Wye Valley are just a few of its **treasures**. But Wales is also famous for its 500 or more castles. Of particular interest are the castles built by King Edward I of England in the 13th century in North Wales. He built these impressive fortifications to protect his newly colonised lands from any Welsh rebellions. The castles of Beaumaris, Harlech, Caenarfon, and Conwy have together been made a UNESCO World Heritage Site.

It was this same King Edward I who, in 1301, began the tradition of **investing** the **heir** to the British **throne** with the **title** of Prince of Wales. This was when he **awarded** the title to his son, the future King Edward II. The **current** Prince of Wales, Prince Charles, was invested by the Queen at a ceremony held in Caernarfon Castle. Charles made speeches in both English and Welsh, but in his speeches he did not include the Welsh village with the longest place name in Europe: Llanfairpwllgwyngyllgogerychwyrndrobwllllantysiliogogogoch. It was probably too hard for him to **pronounce**, but why don't you try?

Beaumaris Castle, regarded as one of the finest examples of medieval castle building.

Notes Snowdonia National Park「スノードニア国立公園」 the Gower peninsula「ガウアー半島」 Wye Valley「ワイ渓谷」 King Edward I エドワード1世（在位1272-1307） fortifications「要塞」 colonised「植民地化された」 rebellions「反乱」 UNESCO World Heritage Site「ユネスコ世界遺産」 King Edward II エドワード2世（在位1307-1327） Queen「女王」ここではエリザベス2世のこと。 Llanfairpwllgwyngyllgogerychwyrndrobwllllantysiliogogogoch「[地名] ランヴァイル・プルグウィンギル・ゴゲリフウィルンドロブル・ランティシリオゴゴゴホ」ウェールズ北部アングルシー島にある。

▶▶▶ 5～7ページ、および73ページのコラムも参照

Reading Comprehension

本文の内容に合わせて、質問の答えとして正しいものを選択肢から選びましょう。

1. Why did King Edward I build castles in North Wales?
   a. Because he wanted to colonise new lands
   b. Because he wanted to defend his territory
   c. Because he liked impressive fortresses

2. Who was the first heir to the British throne to be given the title of Prince of Wales?
   a. The son of King Edward I
   b. Prince Charles
   c. King Edward I

3. According to the writer, why did Prince Charles not mention the name of the Welsh village in his speeches?
   a. Because he can't speak Welsh
   b. Because he is heir to the British throne
   c. Because he probably found it too difficult to pronounce

Writing Exercises

本章中で使われている表現を参考にして、以下の英文を完成させましょう。

1. この公園はバラで有名です。
   This park is _____ _____ its roses.

2. 2〜3日休みを取ったらどうですか。
   Why _____ _____ take a few days off?

3. 次の同窓会でお会いするのを楽しみにしています。
   I'm _____ forward to _____ _____ at the next class reunion.

4. この部屋は、100人までの学生に十分なスペースがあります。
   This room _____ enough space for _____ _____ a hundred students.

Day 13

Don't You Know that UK Designs Are Popular?

カッコイイだけにあらず、ブリティッシュ・スタイル

今日のタケシが身に着けているのは、人気のブリティッシュ・デザイン。
ユニオンジャックを使っただけのものから、
高級デザイナーズブランドまで、チョイスはさまざま。
でも、クールなそのスタイルの背景に、
悪条件で労働者を働かせる環境があったとしたら？
そして、華やかな衣料品産業で注目を集めるエコ・ファッションとは？

Listen to the Dialogue

DL 67　CD 67

会話文の音声を聞いて、空所に適切な語を書き入れましょう。
完成したら、ペアになって会話の練習をしてみましょう。

Chris: Eh! You're wearing a sweater with a 1._____ _____ design!

Takeshi: Yes. I went to Camden Market, which has become a must-see 2._____ _____, and I found it there. What do you think?

Chris: It looks great, but I'm a bit surprised that you bought such a sweater.

Takeshi: Didn't you know that the Union Jack 3._____ is incredibly popular in Japan?

Chris: No, I didn't.

Takeshi: You can see it on lots of goods, from bags and socks to T-shirts and even 4._____-_____ covers.

Chris: I had no idea.

Takeshi: It became even 5._____ _____ after William and Kate's wedding and the London Olympics.

Chris: I see. The Japanese also have a soft spot for British brands 6._____ _____ Vivienne Westwood, Burberry, and Paul Smith, right?

Takeshi: Yes, we love them.

Notes Camden Market「カムデン・マーケット」ロンドン中心部にあり、服飾品、靴などの店や屋台が並ぶ。　must-see「必見の」　have a soft spot for「〜が好きである」　Vivienne Westwood　ヴィヴィアン・ウエストウッド　Burberry 1856年トーマス・バーバリーによって創立された服飾メーカー。　Paul Smith　ポール・スミス

▶▶ 50ページの『本書に登場する人名・団体名』も参照

Expressions for Everyday English

Don't you ＋動詞の原形？「〜ではないのですか」

否定語が文頭に置かれる否定疑問文です。確認したい時、あるいは意外に思ったり失望したりした時に使われます。この疑問文に対する答えは、Yes「いいえ」、No「はい」となります。日本語の「はい／いいえ」に影響されないようにしましょう。

DL 68　CD 68

Don't you like music?　あなたは音楽が好きではないのですか。
　　Yes, I do.　いいえ、好きです。　No, I don't.　はい、好きではありません。
Don't we have to be at the restaurant by seven?
　　　　　　　　7時までにレストランに着いてなくちゃいけないんじゃないの？
Doesn't he remember the accident?　彼はあの事故を覚えていないの？
Didn't you think it was strange?　変だと思わなかったのですか。

Let's Try!
学習した表現を使って自由に英文を作り、ペアになって会話をしてみましょう。
A: Don't you ＿＿＿＿＿＿＿＿＿＿＿？　＿＿＿＿＿＿＿＿＿＿＿ですか。
B: ＿＿＿＿＿＿＿＿＿＿＿．　＿＿＿＿＿＿＿＿＿＿＿。

Useful Vocabulary

DL 69　CD 69

以下は、次ページで学習するトピックに関する重要語句です。
それぞれの語句の意味に当てはまる日本語を、選択肢から選びましょう。

1. come to mind　[　]　　6. labour　[　]
2. industry　[　]　　7. discuss　[　]
3. goods　[　]　　8. ensure　[　]
4. consumer　[　]　　9. wage　[　]
5. aware of　[　]　　10. boring　[　]

　　a. 退屈な　b. 思い浮かぶ　c. 消費者　d. 商品　e. 労働、労力
　　f. 賃金　g. 〜を意識して、〜が分かって　h. 産業
　　i. 〜について論議する　j. 〜を保証する

Day 13　Don't You Know that UK Designs Are Popular?

Reading: Chris's Insight

DL 70 ~ 72 ● CD 70 ~ ● CD 72

British Fashion - You Are What You Wear

When people think of fashion, the first places that **come to mind** are probably France and Italy. However, Britain has always had a thriving fashion **industry**. Did you know that it was
5 British designer Mary Quant who made the miniskirt popular back in the 1960s? Now Britain is considered to be a highly creative and exciting fashion centre. Designers like Vivienne Westwood, Paul Smith, Stella McCartney, and
10 Victoria Beckham are recognised internationally, and their fashion **goods** are sold across the globe. Yes, British fashion is hot!

Fashion designer Mary Quant in 1969

Britain is also a world leader in 'ethical' fashion. British **consumers** are becoming more and more **aware of** where and how clothes are made. Topics
15 such as sweatshops and child **labour** are now openly **discussed** in the media. Many consumers no longer buy clothes just because they are cheap. They want to **ensure** that the workers who make the clothes are getting a fair **wage** and have good working conditions.

Many people believe that eco fashion must be **boring** and expensive, but it
20 can actually be very stylish and affordable. Several famous people, like the Duchess of Cambridge, Michelle Obama, and Harry Potter star Emma Watson, often choose ethical fashion. How about you?

Notes thriving「繁栄した」 'ethical' fashion「エシカル（倫理的に正しい）ファッション」原料から製品まで、地球環境に配慮し発展途上国の適正労働条件のもと生産される衣料。 sweatshop「労働搾取工場」 affordable「手頃な、無理なく買える価格の」 the Duchess of Cambridge ケンブリッジ公爵夫人 Michelle Obama ミシェル・オバマ。第44代米国大統領バラク・オバマの妻。 Emma Watson エマ・ワトソン。女優。

▶▶ 72ページの『本書に登場する人名・団体名』も参照

Reading Comprehension

本文の内容に合わせて、質問の答えとして正しいものを選択肢から選びましょう。

1. How is Britain's fashion industry considered?
    a. It is better than the French or Italian fashion industries
    b. It has been very popular since the 1960s
    c. It is original and exciting

2. Why are many British consumers interested in ethical fashion?
    a. Because they want to buy cheap clothes
    b. Because they are concerned about the working conditions in some clothing factories
    c. Because the media often advertises eco fashion

3. What is the general image of eco fashion?
    a. Dull and overpriced
    b. Trendy and reasonably priced
    c. Unpopular among famous people

Writing Exercises

本章中で使われている表現を参考にして、以下の英文を完成させましょう。

1. その店は、ペンから卵まで、なんでも売っています。
    The shop sells everything _____ pens _____ eggs.

2. 彼らは言葉がもつ力に気付いていません。
    They are not _____ _____ the power of language.

3. 彼女は優秀な医者だと考えられています。
    She _____ _____ to _____ an excellent doctor.

4. 彼が昨日ここで会ったのは、何とケイトだったのよ。
    _____ was Kate _____ he met here yesterday.

Day 14

Would You Like to See a Play?
英語は詩人シェイクスピアに学べ

イギリスの大劇作家、シェイクスピア。
500年を経た今でも、その作品は世界中の人々を魅了し続け、
彼が残した言葉は、私たちの中で広く使われています。
クリス先生とタケシは、イギリス中部にあるシェイクスピアの生まれ故郷、
ストラトフォード・アポン・エイヴォンに到着しました。
明日は、蜂蜜色の建築物で知られるコッツウォルズに向かいます。

Listen to the Dialogue

DL 73 CD 73

会話文の音声を聞いて、空所に適切な語を書き入れましょう。
完成したら、ペアになって会話の練習をしてみましょう。

Chris: A visit to Britain would not be ¹._____ without a trip to Stratford-upon-Avon.

Takeshi: Yes, ²._____ _____ wonderful to be in William Shakespeare's birthplace. Actually, my university's drama club put on *Hamlet* last year.

Chris: Would you like to see a play?

Takeshi: That would ³._____ _____.

Chris: OK. I'll see if I can get tickets.

Takeshi: And do you know ⁴._____ _____ I would like to do?

Chris: No, tell me.

Takeshi: Well, I'd love to have a traditional English cream tea.

Chris: Ah, so you like scones with clotted cream and jam, eh?

Takeshi: ⁵._____ _____! The Brits are not the only ones with a sweet tooth!

Chris: OK. Let's go to the Cotswolds tomorrow. It's the ⁶._____ _____ for a cream tea.

Takeshi: Mmm... I can't wait!

Notes clotted cream「クロテッド・クリーム」乳脂肪分を55〜60％まで高めた濃厚なクリーム。
ones with a sweet tooth「甘いもの好きな人たち」　the Cotswolds「コッツウォルズ」ロンドンの北西部に広がる丘陵地帯。

▶▶▶ 5、7ページも参照

Expressions for Everyday English

Would you like to ＋動詞の原形？「～したいですか」

相手の希望を尋ねる時、または控え目に相手の意向を質問する時の表現です。Do you want to ~？と同じ内容ですが、より丁寧な印象になります。また、Would you like ＋名詞（句）は、「～はいかがですか」と相手に何かを勧める表現になります。

🎧 DL 74　💿 CD 74

Would you like to leave a message?　ご伝言いたしましょうか。(伝言を残したいですか)
Would you like to go to a movie?　映画を見にいきませんか。
Would you like to try that on?　[店員から客に] そちらをご試着なさいますか。
Would you like some more tea?　お茶をもう少しいかがですか。[名詞句]

Let's Try!

学習した表現を使って自由に英文を作り、ペアになって会話をしてみましょう。

A: Would you like to _____？ _____ですか。
B: Yes, I'd love to.　ええ、喜んで。

Useful Vocabulary

🎧 DL 75　💿 CD 75

以下は、次ページで学習するトピックに関する重要語句です。
それぞれの語句の意味に当てはまる日本語を、選択肢から選びましょう。

1. figure　　　[　]
2. literature　[　]
3. redesign　　[　]
4. audience　　[　]
5. massive　　 [　]
6. drama　　　 [　]
7. widen　　　 [　]
8. vocabulary　[　]
9. noun　　　　[　]
10. adjective　[　]

a. 人物　**b.** (非常に) 大きな　**c.** 語彙　**d.** 観客
e. ～を設計し直す　**f.** 形容詞　**g.** 文学　**h.** 名詞　**i.** ～を拡大する
j. 劇、戯曲

Reading: Chris's Insight

DL 76, 77　CD 76　CD 77

You Speak Like Shakespeare!

Who has not heard of William Shakespeare? He is widely considered to be the greatest *figure* in English *literature*. Because of this, he is affectionately referred to as 'The Bard'. His plays were written over 500 years ago, but they are still as popular as ever across the world. Stratford, where Shakespeare was born, is the home of the Royal Shakespeare Company, or RSC. The Company's theatres have recently been totally *redesigned*. The actors are now much closer to the *audience*, so you can enjoy performances of Shakespeare's plays even more.

Royal Shakespeare Theatre and Swan Theatre in Stratford

Everyone recognises the *massive* impact Shakespeare had on English *drama*. Many people can no doubt remember famous lines from Shakespeare's plays, such as *Hamlet*'s 'To be, or not to be, that is the question'. But far fewer people realise the fact that he *widened* the English *vocabulary*, creating over 1,500 new words. *Nouns* like design, addiction, and manager, as well as *adjectives* like fashionable, soft-hearted, and worthless, were all used for the first time by Shakespeare. English speakers almost certainly use some of the Bard's words every day! If you want to learn more about Shakespeare, it's easy, as there are over 150 million pages about him on Google. Enjoy!

Notes　the Bard「シェイクスピア」the Bard of Avonという場合もある。　as popular as ever「相変わらず人気で」　the Royal Shakespeare Company「ロイヤル・シェイクスピア・カンパニー」ストラトフォードを拠点にする劇団。　even more「さらに、一層」　lines「(役者の) セリフ」　'To be, or not to be, that is the question'「生きるべきか死ぬべきか、それが問題だ」シェイクスピア作*Hamlet*第3幕第1場でのハムレットのセリフ。　soft-hearted「心優しい」

Reading Comprehension

本文の内容に合わせて、質問の答えとして正しいものを選択肢から選びましょう。

1. Why is Shakespeare referred to as 'The Bard'?
    a. Because his plays are over 500 years old
    b. Because he is respected as the greatest writer in English literature
    c. Because everyone has heard of him

2. Why have RSC performances of Shakespeare's plays become more enjoyable?
    a. Because RSC audiences are now in closer contact with the actors
    b. Because the RSC is in Shakespeare's birthplace
    c. Because the RSC theatres needed to be redesigned

3. What is not so well known about Shakespeare?
    a. He had a great influence on English drama
    b. Lots of information about him can be found on Google
    c. He contributed many new words to the English language

Writing Exercises

本章中で使われている表現を参考にして、以下の英文を完成させましょう。

1. 我々は植物がなかったら、生きていけません。
   We cannot survive _____ plants.

2. 来週、初めてスキーに行きます。
   I'll go skiing _____ the first _____ next week.

3. この山岳リゾートは、冬だけでなく夏も人気があります。
   This mountain resort is popular in summer _____ _____ as in winter.

4. 彼女が微笑みかけてくれたことで希望を持てました。
   The _____ _____ she smiled at me gave _____ hope.

Day 15 That's the Great Thing about Travel!

変わりゆくイギリス王室

楽しかった15日間のイギリスの旅も、今日で終わり。
たくさんのことを学んだ旅の終わりに、
タケシは日本では絶対に見られない「王室モノ」のお土産を購入するようです。
複雑な歴史を抱えながら変化を遂げ、
その国民に広く愛される立場となったイギリス王室。
21世紀の王室は、ますます身近な存在になりそうです。

Listen to the Dialogue

DL 78　CD 78

会話文の音声を聞いて、空所に適切な語を書き入れましょう。
完成したら、ペアになって会話の練習をしてみましょう。

Chris: Well, your visit to the UK is ¹_____ _____. Time flies, right?

Takeshi: It sure does. But I had ²_____ _____.

Chris: You certainly packed a lot into a short ³_____ _____ time.

Takeshi: That's true. And I learnt so much about British life and culture.

Chris: That's the great thing ⁴_____ _____. It really does broaden the mind.

Takeshi: Well, I don't know how to thank you enough for all you've done for me, Chris.

Chris: It's been my pleasure, Takeshi. ⁵_____ _____ say you wanted to buy some souvenirs?

Takeshi: Yes. I was thinking of buying royal family souvenirs – some mugs, magnets, shortbread biscuits...

Chris: Really?

Takeshi: Yes, because for Japanese people, it's very unusual to see pictures of royalty on ⁶_____ _____.

Chris: I see. Well, let's go shopping!

Notes souvenirs「記念品、みやげ物」　shortbread biscuits「ショートブレッド・ビスケット」スコットランドの伝統的な菓子。　royalty「王室(の人々)」

Expressions for Everyday English

I was thinking of -ing「～しようと思っていたんだ」

考えていたことを明らかにする表現です。前置詞 of の後は動名詞(-ing)がきます。通常、think は進行形にはできませんが、この場合は「考える」という状態ではなく、継続的な動作を示す動詞なので、進行形になります。

🎧 DL 79　💿 CD 79

I was thinking of tidying up my bedroom.　寝室を片付けようと思ってたのよ。
I was thinking of going to Tokyo Disneyland.
　　　　　　　　　　　　東京ディズニーランドに行こうと思ってたんだ。
I was thinking of watering the plants.　植木に水をやろうと思ってたの。
I was just thinking of calling you.　ちょうど君に電話しようと思っていたんだ。

Let's Try!

学習した表現を使って自由に英文を作り、ペアになって会話をしてみましょう。

A: Do you have any plans for the weekend?　週末の予定は？
B: I was thinking of ＿＿＿＿＿＿＿. ＿＿＿＿＿＿＿しようと思ってたんだ。

Useful Vocabulary

🎧 DL 80　💿 CD 80

以下は、次ページで学習するトピックに関する重要語句です。
それぞれの語句の意味に当てはまる日本語を、選択肢から選びましょう。

1. monarchy　　　[　　]
2. undergo　　　 [　　]
3. propose　　　 [　　]
4. reform　　　　[　　]
5. depend on　　 [　　]
6. put an end to　[　　]
7. boost　　　　　[　　]
8. appreciate　　 [　　]
9. fond of　　　　[　　]
10. humanise　　 [　　]

> **a.** ～を提案する　**b.** ～に人間味を与える　**c.** ～を高く評価する
> **d.** ～を経験する　**e.** ～次第である、～による
> **f.** ～を促進させる・高める　**g.** ～が好きで、～を好んで
> **h.** ～に終止符を打つ　**i.** 改正　**j.** 君主制

Day 15　That's the Great Thing about Travel!

Reading: Chris's Insight

Historic Changes to the British Monarchy

The United Kingdom has had a single **monarchy** system since 1603, when King James VI of Scotland became King James I of England. Over the last 400 years, the monarchy has **undergone** many changes. Recently, the Prime Minister **proposed** a **reform** of the laws of succession to the British throne. The Succession to the Crown Act was given Royal Assent on 25 April, 2013, thus making it law. The new law means that succession to the British crown no longer **depends on** the gender of the first-born child. Supporters believe that it **puts an end to** centuries of discrimination against women and brings the monarchy more in line with the reality of 21st-century Britain.

William and Kate's wedding also helped give the royal family a 21st-century image and **boosted** its popularity right across the world. Around two billion people watched the wedding on TV. Many Brits **appreciate** the fact that William married a commoner with no royal blood. They have also become very **fond of** Princes William and Harry because they come across as being very 'normal'. It doesn't hurt, of course, that they are the sons of the most popular royal family member ever, Princess Diana! All this has done a great deal to '**humanise**' this special family.

Prince William and his wife Catherine at the Chapel Royal in St James's Palace on the christening of their baby son Prince George

Notes King James VI of Scotland, King James I of England スコットランド王ジェームズ6世（在位1567-1625）、イングランド王・アイルランド王ジェームズ1世（在位1603-1625）。 succession「継承」 The Succession to the Crown Act「王位継承法」王位継承の先後を性別によらないものに改めた法律。 Royal Assent「国王の裁可」 brings ~ in line with...「～を…に一致させる」 commoner「(貴族・皇族に対して)一般人」 come across as...「～として受け入れられている」 Princes William and Harry ウィリアム王子とヘンリー王子 It dosen't hurt = It really helps「大いに役立つ、うまく影響する」 Princess Diana ダイアナ妃

▶▶▶ 72ページの『本書に登場する人名・団体名』も参照

Reading Comprehension

本文の内容に合わせて、質問の答えとして正しいものを選択肢から選びましょう。

1. What has happened to the British monarchy since 1603?
   a. It has changed from having a King of England to a King of Scotland
   b. It has experienced a lot of changes
   c. It has doubled in the United Kingdom

2. What was the main purpose of the Succession to the Crown Act?
   a. To gain Royal Assent
   b. To support the Prime Minister's proposal
   c. To bring gender equality to the succession to the throne

3. What has NOT helped increase the royal family's popularity and 'humanness'?
   a. The fact that Princes William and Harry are brothers
   b. The fact that Princes William and Harry act in a 'normal' manner
   c. The fact that Princes William and Harry are Princess Diana's sons

Writing Exercises

本章中で使われている表現を参考にして、以下の英文を完成させましょう。

1. 人々は自分の健康をとても意識するようになりました。
   People have _____ very conscious of their health.

2. 彼の家族は脂っこい食べ物が大好きです。
   His family _____ very _____ _____ fatty foods.

3. 駅へどう行けばいいか教えてくれませんか。
   Can _____ tell me _____ _____ get to the station?

4. そのニュースはインターネットを介してすぐに世界中に広まりました。
   The news spread quickly _____ the _____ through the Internet.

Names of People & Groups

本書に登場する人名・団体名③

Day 13

Mary Quant
マリー・クワント（1934-　）
　ファッションデザイナー、ファッションブランドの名称。1960年代後半からのミニスカートの世界的流行はマリー・クワントから始まったとされ、ファッション産業への多大な貢献が認められている。

Stella McCartney
ステラ・マッカートニー（1971-　）
　ファッションデザイナー、ファッションブランドの名称。ビートルズのポール・マッカートニーの娘である。厳格な菜食主義者として知られ、自らのブランドにおいても革や毛皮を使用しない。

Victoria Beckham
ヴィクトリア・ベッカム（1974-　）
　歌手、ファッションデザイナー、ファッションブランドの名称。女性グループのスパイス・ガールズのメンバーで、夫はサッカー選手のデービッド・ベッカム。

the Duchess of Cambridge
ケンブリッジ公爵夫人（1982-　）
　イギリス王室のケンブリッジ公ウィリアム王子の妻。一般家庭の出身で、ウィリアム王子とはセント・アンドルーズ大学での学友だった。結婚前からそのファッションが注目を集めている。

Michelle Obama
ミシェル・オバマ（1964-　）
　第44代アメリカ大統領夫人。180cmの長身を活かしたファッションは常に注目の的で、アメリカピープル誌の「今年の女性ベスト・ドレッサー10人」などにも選出されている。

Emma Watson
エマ・ワトソン（1990-　）
　映画『ハリー・ポッター』シリーズに出演。バーバリーなどの広告のモデルを務める他、フェアトレードのファッション・ブランドにも関わっている。

Day 14

William Shakespeare
ウィリアム・シェイクスピア（1564-1616）
　詩人、劇作家。その作品が現在でも世界中で愛されている。個人として英語に最も影響を与えた人物とも、また、今の英語の原型を作り上げたとも言われている。"All's well that ends well"「終わりよければ全てよし」、"love is blind"「恋は盲目」など、現在もなお使われている名言も多い。

Day 15

King James VI of Scotland, King James I of England
スコットランド王ジェームズ6世（在位1567-1625）、イングランド・アイルランド王ジェームズ1世（在位1603-1625）
　1603年に女王エリザベス1世が死去すると、スコットランド王ジェームズ6世はジェームズ1世としてイングランドとアイルランドの王を兼任することになった。以降、イングランドとスコットランドは1707年に合同してグレートブリテン王国になり、1801年にはアイルランド王国と合同し、グレートブリテンおよびアイルランド連合王国となった。

Princess Diana
ウェールズ公妃ダイアナ（1961-1997）
　ウェールズ公チャールズの最初の妃。1981年にチャールズ皇太子と結婚し、ウィリアム王子とヘンリー王子をもうけたものの、1996年に離婚。翌年パリで交通事故により不慮の死を遂げる。存命中から、その行動から服装までのすべてが注目の的であったが、死後もなお、イギリス国民の絶大な人気を誇っている。また、エイズ問題や地雷除去問題などの慈善事業にも積極的取り組み、社会に大きな影響を与えた。

Let's Talk about the UK!
英国コラム③

ブラックキャブ、ダブルデッカーを乗りこなそう！
Day 11 I Guess I Should Have a Black-Cab Experience より

　ロンドンに行ったらぜひ一度は乗ってみたいのがタクシーとバス。どちらもロンドンの風景の一部となり、ポストカードやお土産品にもイラストや写真が使われています。タクシーはブラックキャブと呼ばれ、赤や黄色など黒以外の車体もありますが、今でも同じ愛称で呼ばれています。車体の天井が高くなっているのは、19世紀から20世紀初頭にかけ、イギリス紳士がシルクハットをかぶったまま乗り込んだ名残り。フロントガラスの上にある「TAXI」のライトの表示が目印です。自動ドアはないので、自分でドアを開閉します。また料金は基本的に現金のみで、車を降りてから支払います。

　タクシーの運転手になるために必要なThe Knowledgeの試験は、ロンドン公共運送業局（Public Carriage Office）が実施しており、合格者は試験の点数によってロンドン全域を運転できる「グリーンバッジ」か、ロンドン近郊の一部分の地域だけを担当できる「イエローバッジ」に認定されます。

　一方、ロンドンでバスと言えば、赤い2階建てのバス、ダブルデッカー。すべてのバス停に必ず止まるバスと、乗降の意思を示さないと停車しない「リクエストストップ」のバスがあります。どちらも手を前に出して運転手に合図を送り、停まったら前から乗車して料金を払います。2階では立ったまま乗ることはできません。降りる時は車内のボタンを押して知らせ、中央のドアから降車します。

　ブラックキャブもダブルデッカーも、乗りこなすには多少の知識と慣れが必要ですが、ぜひ一度乗ってみましょう。また違ったロンドンの景色が見えるかもしれません。ちなみにアメリカやフランスでは左側に運転席があるのが一般的ですが、イギリスは日本と同じ右側にあり、車道も左側通行です。

プリンス・オブ・ウェールズって、結局どこの王子様？
Day 12 I'm Looking forward to Seeing Wales! より

　「プリンス・オブ・ウェールズ」という言葉を聞いたことがあるでしょうか。現在では、チャールズ皇太子がこの称号を有しています。なぜチャールズ皇太子は「ウェールズの王子（正式にはウェールズ大公）」と呼ばれるのでしょうか。「プリンス・オブ・イングランド」ではないのでしょうか。

　Day 1でも触れているように、イギリスはイングランド、ウェールズ、スコットランド、北アイルランドの4つの地域から成り立っています。さかのぼること約800年前、イングランドのエドワード1世はウェールズに侵攻しました。イングランドは戦いに勝利しましたが、ウェールズ人の反感を抑えるために、王妃のエリナーをウェールズに住まわせ、その地で生まれた王子に、ウェールズの君主として「プリンス・オブ・ウェールズ」の称号を与えました。これによってエドワード1世は、この王子がウェールズの支配者であることを国民に納得させたのです。皇太子となった後のエドワード2世はウェールズの君主であり、同時に次のイングランド王を約束されたことになりました。以降、この形で王位継承が行われ、皇太子は「プリンス・オブ・ウェールズ」と名乗る習慣ができたのです。

　エドワード1世は、それまで国政に際して使われていたフランス語を英語に変えたり、北方のスコットランドの征服を計画したり、その遠征の戦費のための増税を認めさせるために1295年の模範議会を召集したりしました。その他、以後700年あまり続く多くの法令を作るなど、現在のイギリスの原型を作った王とも言われています。

本書には CD（別売）があります

Let's Check Out the UK!
マクベイ先生と行くイギリスを知る15日間の旅

2015年1月20日　初版第 1 刷発行
2025年2月20日　初版第14刷発行

著　者　　Paul Chris McVay
　　　　　川　田　伸　道

発行者　　福　岡　正　人
発行所　　株式会社　金　星　堂
（〒101-0051）東京都千代田区神田神保町 3-21
Tel. (03) 3263-3828（営業部）
(03) 3263-3997（編集部）
Fax (03) 3263-0716
https://www.kinsei-do.co.jp

編集担当　松本明子　　　　　　　　　　Printed in Japan
印刷所・製本所／倉敷印刷株式会社

本書の無断複製・複写は著作権法上での例外を除き禁じられています。
本書を代行業者等の第三者に依頼してスキャンやデジタル化することは、たとえ個人や家庭内での利用であっても認められておりません。
落丁・乱丁本はお取り替えいたします。

ISBN978-4-7647-4000-6　C1082